THE LAZINESS GENE

JOHN D. COLLINS

DEDICATION

This book is dedicated to my amazing parents, Des and Val. Thank you for everything you have done for me.

CONTENTS

ACKNOWLEDGMENTS

A special thanks to Rola and Brona, I am forever grateful for your help and support. Thanks to Sophie, Andrew and Brian who were constant sources of inspiration and motivation.

1 INTRODUCTION

Why write a book about decision making, logic, laziness and the conscious mind? For too long I have drifted through life, rolling from one day to the next just working, eating, watching tv until my evitable demise. I think what really got me was the day I realized I was racing home from work to do the thing that I truly loved, watch TV. This was my laziness gene kicking in, it was dominating my life, making all my decisions. For a period of my life my favorite hobby was TV, whether I liked it or not this was my 'passion'. I wasn't here when it was on, I would be in a semi trance state between the TV and phone screen. I was passing the hours until I slept. I was lazy. Lazy is not living.

The everyday can be extraordinary. Let's say you work 260 days a year, those are the days that shouldn't be lost in your life story. That is why I wrote this, to prove to myself I could write a book only on those 'normal' workdays. I am not some Millionaire writing from my mansion in Bora Bora telling you to follow your 'passion' and how to be happy. I am on a mission to take charge of my 'normal' life, making the 'normal' wonderful and sharing with you my thoughts along the way.

So, who am I? Who is this person dishing out all the advice? At time of writing I am 37 years old married man employed as high school Mathematics teacher in an International Baccalaureate school, also I am an Author with some other projects in the pipeline. Formerly, I was Head of Physical Education in a school in Ireland. I am a sports coach and have written previously about sports psychology when in college. Most of all I am constantly changing, I am always trying to learn and trying to just get a little better every day at whatever I am doing. I am trying not to be lazy.

How do I have time to do everything I say I do in this book? Well that's the point of the book, I didn't think I had this time or the energy to anything other than work and relax. Work was necessary for money and once it was done the metaphorical laziness gene took over. My laziness had me convinced that I deserved to relax all the time, laziness is an addictive state, it is a comfortable cocoon that is so hard to shake. Laziness was leading me to a wasted life.

I was letting my laziness take charge of my life is it in charge of your life? Your inherent lazy gene will make the decisions if you don't become more conscious of it. These decisions are who you are without you even realizing it. You are the product of your everyday choices. My choice to do nothing every day was ruining my life. I needed to change that. This book shows you what I have learnt (successes and some mistakes) along the way. The main thing I have learned is that it is possible to make every ordinary day better when you take charge and make the decisions. Are you where I was not so long ago? Are you dominated by the laziness gene? It might be time to change a few aspects of your life to make your everyday just a little more extraordinary. This could make your life more fulfilled and your mind more satisfied. That is what this book is trying to help you achieve. Become a more conscious you, that is the antidote to the laziness. Every single day matters, your time is precious, try not to waste it.

Are you drifting to your death too or are you here? Be here now in this world. It is such a wonderful gift you have been given, life. No matter what your story, you are alive, what a magical thing. This is your one chance, your one shot at this. Is a life that is not lived to the fullest, an unconscious drift through it, a waste of your chance. Do we have a responsibility to all those who don't live to achieve? We had a one in trillion chance, the other billions who didn't become you, they are still in the nothingness. Even if you believe in the afterlife do your beliefs stop you from being amazing in this life? Alternatively, why even bother to be informed? Drift through life in an unconscious cocoon, ignorance is bliss. The choice is yours.

Maybe think about the world after your ultimate demise--what have you left to show for it? Maybe you will have left an epic ass groove in the spot on the couch you always sit in but that, I am afraid, no matter how epic, it will be forgotten. Your life will at some stage be forgotten the same as you may have forgotten your great great grandfather. Maybe you can do something with your life to make your future generations remember you, hopefully more Albert Einstein and Mozart than the Genghis Khan type of legacy but that isn't what I am getting at. The first person you need to impress is yourself; you are the person who cares most about you and what you achieve. But really your life isn't about legacy; life is about living it. It is pointless to be remembered if you hated every minute of the life that got you there. Is a miserable 'successful' life better than an 'unsuccessful' happy life? This leads us to the measure of success. How do we measure success? It seems to be the accumulation of material and wealth. An artist who doesn't get the big bucks for his paintings is deemed unsuccessful. That same artist lives in a modest cabin on a lake, waking up every morning surrounded by beauty and without any pressures of a modern working day. He is happy. Is he then deemed a failure in your mind? If you chase wealth to find happiness, this will be something you will pass onto your children. Your children will see their parents strive for wealth instead of spending time on things that bring true happiness. The curse of wealth over mental health will be the legacy you could give them.

The legacy you could leave--if you have children or are going to have children--is that they are happy and set up to enjoy their life when you are not around. They will be inspired by you if you are conscious in each day. Children learn by what you do not what you say. If your demeanor is shy, and your child is shy because of it, there is no use in being frustrated that they are not more outgoing. They have learned to be shy, not through any words but by observing your interactions. You may condition your children with your actions whether you like it or not. If you are lazy, your children will imitate. Can you make your actions match the person you want your child to be?

Your everyday choices mold you into the person you are. Being conscious of these decisions is crucial to being someone you are proud of. Being a person you are proud of is an amazing feeling. The aim of this book is to open the reader's eyes so they can awaken in the conscious world. Ugh, that sounds so bloody pretentious, I will try again. The aim of this book is just maybe to make the reader aware they can have more input into their own day to day life than they currently have, through a more conscious mindset avoiding the temptation to slip into lazy mode.

Every moment, reaction and experience are in some way controllable by a conscious you. We drift through life with our faces buried in the cellphone and screens until we realize that we fucked up and we should have been more conscious earlier. It's all linked to your attitude. Your attitude is controllable by a conscious you. The unconscious you will check your phone every 5 minutes, will eat the cookies, watching endless hours of TV and will lie in bed when not tired. The conscious you can decide to implement a plan to just be a slightly better you every day until you come an amazing you. Striving for but not necessarily reaching 'the best you', because that puts a limit on your potential. Your potential does not have a limit, you impose your own limits unconsciously, now might be the time to be conscious of your lack of limits.

Later, we discuss the practicalities of conscious living but not necessarily an in-depth look into human consciousness. In a way a guide to experiencing life through more awareness in your conscious and unconscious decisions. Someone who works for a living and has limited downtime with family and responsibilities must make some practical decisions; each one can set them on a path to a slightly more awesome or a slightly less awesome life. That is where consciousness must come in. This book comes from a person that wishes to be a fully conscious and mindful human not someone who is in an amazing Zen place. I have more faults that I care to list, one of which is a tendency to be lazy during free time, but I am aware of many of them and have been consciously trying to improve myself through the steps throughout the book. I've learned through both my successes and failures, but I have used my time more productively than ever before, leading to my satisfaction with myself.

You can make decisions today that can facilitate changes in your life for the better. Let's face it we all know that correct diet, more exercise, more reading, fewer screens, more creating and positive mindset are better for us. How do we implement this? My life is tiring, and I lack energy and focus when I have my own time. The reasons you don't do these things are linked to the fact you don't do these things. Confused, right? You have no energy because you don't exercise. You don't create because you don't create. The excuses you can come up with can only be told to yourself, if you are genuinely enjoying the lack of challenge you are one of the few. People say that life needs purpose. Don't have the only purpose in your life as your job, especially not if you work in a job that you don't particularly enjoy. Do things that make you a doer, then you are a doer. More on this in chapter 5.

The hardest three words to say are 'I don't know.' It strikes a humble chord that doesn't sit well with our ego. Becoming well versed in any field of knowledge requires the 'conscious you' to continue to set your answer at 'I don't know'. Finding questions that you don't know the answer to and then following that path continuously on rotation. I am not writing that I know the best path for you, but I intend to inspire you to ask yourself questions. What is your standard answer? For example, are you prepared to say 'I don't know' when someone asks you a question at a party? Or do you give some vague answer with large words to seem impressive as some sort of pillar of knowledge? Do you listen to other opinions that disagree with yours and then think that they are wrong, or do you think that you need to research what they have talked about before you can discuss it further? Without doubt, my ego gets the better of me when this situation comes up; I can have my belief that I am right, but not the humility to think I could be wrong because I don't know all the facts. I need to work on changing this, do you?

Who gets more attention on Instagram--the person who is an overnight expert in nutrition and posts a 200 summary of it #vegan #keto #livingmybestlife or someone who writes a well-researched, evidenced based and clinically trialed paper on the topic of nutritional benefits of a vegan or Keto diet? That's a problem really, isn't it? The celebrity who has something to sell along with their newly found nutritional knowledge is the next level of this. The society we live seems to value this type of 'content' above most, I hope the tide is turning, but just take a wander through social media and see who gets the most followers. On the topic of social media, is it possible to do anything in this world anymore without sharing? Can't we just enjoy our lives? More on this in chapter 8.

When you read this book hopefully you will think about how you can spend your time. A little bit more productivity on a consistent basis can lead to long term satisfaction. Goals, habits, routines, experiences, and attitude come together in a conscious mix where you control your days. Maybe you have far more choices in your life than you are currently aware of. Your downtime is not for enjoying SpongeBob SquarePants. It could be for enjoying your education and your creativity. Your car journeys could be a sounding board or a mental mind map for your ideas instead of a mind-numbing experience. More on this is chapter 2.

What goes on in your head is different than everyone else's. You haven't a clue what your own mother or brother are thinking never mind what a stranger of completely different upbringing is thinking and going through. I am not presuming to know what is going on in yours or others' consciousness, this would put me deep in false consensuses bias where I think that everyone thinks and has the same opinions as I. I can, however, open my consciousness to you so you can use these examples. Maybe then you can open your consciousness and use it in ways to make choices that might help you. People's egos make them think they are right, and people's false consensus bias ensures that they think most people agree with them. I am aware of this so feel free to disagree and let me know, I am willing and ready to learn. Whether I succeed in remaining unbiased and free of ego is up to the reader to answer. It is highly unlikely that I manage to get through writing this book without in some way allowing my ego to influence what is said. As I am conscious of it, I then can address it and try not let my ego take me and the reader on a trip of self-satisfaction and smugness.

Let's get on with it then, let's make some conscious choices, lets avoid laziness and let's be aware of some of the unconscious traps and general day to day bullshit that can fill our days.

2 IS TV WORTH IT?

Another day over, you are home from work, you switch on a screen and ahhhh, relax. What a day. A real mental struggle to get up early, go to work, ten solid hours working for 'the man', now it's home time and you walk in the door ready to relax because the day is done. Time to be lazy.

The day is done is such a dangerous mindset for a person who is conscious about living. You limit your doing part of the day to your workday. The work part of the day is for most of us where we are working for someone else. To switch off when you are not getting paid to do something is the industrial revolution dream, you are resting now so you can give your all to work the next day. Be aware of a life of a minion; that is what you might become, a little yellow one-eyed minion, literally, no, figuratively, or wait, is literally allowed now when it's not literally? I figuratively don't even know anymore. Literally.

The exhaustion and the fall onto the couch into the routine of poor food choices and screens and then doing it all again the next day on repeat. We can probably all relate to this at some stage of our lives, if not the current stage of who we are. We see screens as our relaxing downtime. We see screens as our get-away from the minion life. I used to love watching TV when I came home from a long day at work. However, we need to see screens as stealing the precious time we have in the world to be more than a couch dweller minion. Mindless screen watching epitomizes laziness.

Are you aware of the negative aspects of screens? Many studies link screens (I take screens here as all forms of the screen watching TV, YouTube, Netflix, Amazon, etc.) with obesity, sleep difficulties, and lower grades in education. But we know this already. The screens we watch are not 'good' for us, but we still watch them, constantly. According to the New York Times report in 2018, Americans on average watch a staggering 5 hours of TV per day on average. With working hours around 9.00am to 6.00pm, a person watching this much TV would lead you to believe a lot of people must be turning on the TV as soon as they arrive in the door home every evening after work. The average American spends pretty much equal time watching TV as they spend at work every week. What time is left for you?

"I just watch my TV to switch off after a tough day" is a usual response to those who seek to defend their obsessions with screens. Think about that statement; if you are switching off when you have time to choose what to do with yourself, when do you switch on? What are the activities you are tuned in for? The work that you do may be the time you see yourself as being 'on'. You must ask yourself to what end does this bring? You are working for someone else following their rules and being productive for them. You are compensated for that use of your time by receiving money in return. Compensation you receive off TV for wasting the rest of your precious time is minimal. It is an escape and a chance to be entertained for a while and you can engage in the Game of Thrones conversation at work. You can avoid the wilderness of the social outcast that comes with 'I can't believe you haven't seen it'. Immediately, I must go home and watch it all, binge watch so I can reply 'yes' at the water cooler and comment on who I think will die in the next episode. How wonderful life is now I can discuss these important issues in Game of Thrones, no longer the social outcast.

The key thing is not to see your free time as time to waste. Using all of it to watch a screen unconsciously is a waste. Your downtime is not the time to fully switch off. When you tune into that series or documentary about someone who is out there doing things, they are switched on, they are doing, you are passive, you are off. Your body and mind are crying out for you to be -

1. present
2. decisive
3. active
4. energetic
5. conscious

Think now of the time you have spent, today, yesterday, this week on screen time. Remember 2 hours a day approximately is 12.5% of your waking year, not to mention the American average of 5 hours TV watching which is 31% of a waking year. Most people only have around 40% of their waking time not accounted for by work, sleep, eating, and commuting. Are you wasting your potential in order to watch these screens? Is the content of the TV show really that important to you that you must continue to do this, day in, day out, until you eventually cease to exist? Remember, and this cannot be contested, you will die, everyone does. Can you genuinely say those hours on Netflix and YouTube were worth it?

Face it, some of us are addicted to laziness; we need new habits, goals, passions. That is what this book is about, our ingrained metaphorical laziness gene. We have an opportunity to live our lives consciously. Watching screens as a matter of routine and boredom is an example of someone drifting through life unconsciously. These people are unaware of the wonder and pure sexiness that life is. Yes, sexiness, yes now.

'The life of a screen addict' would be the most boring film ever. No news to anyone, but the screens we interact with are taking over from the real relationships and real-life experiences. But maybe that is reality now and we should just deal with it. Life is now experienced through screens--we don't need to visit any country because we can watch it. We don't need to taste the food because we can see it. We don't need to play sport because we can live it through the screen. Maybe this is the future. Why bother to take a trip? It is all there on a screen to see, and without the effort or the crowds. I don't need to put my liquids in a clear plastic bag when I can watch a show on Peru. I don't need to sit for 14 hours cramped when I can watch a documentary about Dubai. Easy, next we will have virtual reality to make it more realistic. I can't wait for this, the effort of leaving the house. Why don't I just order in the food then put on the VR mask and eat beside the fake beach instead of experiencing the wind, the sand, the drive and the bugs? That's it, I am convinced--I am never leaving the house again. This is where life becomes something very unsexy. This is where life becomes pretend instead of real.

Are you a TV-watching expert? This is the type of expert that can be referred to as armchair quarterbacks. These people are capable of criticizing those who are experienced in running a restaurant, making furniture, hitting a home run, selling houses, running marathons, baking cakes, and, of course, musical ability from the couch as they munch down the chips. They feel like they can criticize people on TV that they see attempt to do things they have never done. It is much easier to be the TV-watching expert than the real expert the camera is pointing at.

People, as non-conscious lazy humans, watch people try to lose weight instead of losing their own weight and some watch people cook amazing food instead of making their own food. We watch people achieve while we vegetate. Real experts at their craft get out and do, practice and hone their skill over thousands of hours, then become so good that they can make a TV show. Be the expert not the critic. It is entertainment, but if you find yourself criticizing someone on television, Netflix or YouTube, have a good long look at the expert in the mirror and ask yourself are you really in the criticizing position or should you be self-critical first. However of course you can use these experts to inspire you, which is one of the good aspects of watching screens.

Four screen watching strategies

1. Use the screen as an inspiration

Chose people who are experts in something you love. Watch those people who inspire you for short periods, then switch off screens and do something. The screen you watch can be a tool of inspiration. You watch people who deserve your attention. Be aware you are watching to become inspired and to learn. Sometimes for me when I do this, I can descend into binge watching 4 hours of guitarist documentaries before I realize I have fallen into the lazy trap. Damn you lazy gene.

I discuss the social media battle we have on our hands in chapter 2. But think about your Instagram feed--what are you getting when you scroll? Debatable whether much of it has a positive effect on your life, but it could. It doesn't control you; you choose what you select to look at, so make it inspiring. You must have the ability to turn off the screen and do something productive after becoming inspired. This means the screen has become your tool, an agent of productivity.

If at the time I have fitness as part of my weekly or monthly goals and I feel tired and unmotivated to get going on a day, I choose to watch the screen. What I put on the screen must be related to my goals--I watch someone else achieve and succeed in the area I want to achieve and succeed. Usually within ten minutes, I have the screen off and I am ready to go do something for myself.

You should try this. If you do watch TV, use it to fuel your motivation for something else, so you turn off the TV and pursue it. Whether it is exercise, cooking, or music, if you can resist your own passion while someone else is doing it, or talking about it on screen in front of you, I am afraid it doesn't sound like a real passion. Time to find another one. Maybe you are forcing it and need to investigate another path to follow. It is ok to switch and pick up new passions? Why not? Passions are just hobbies at one point. Passion is just a fancy word for shit that humans really like to do. How did anyone start a new hobby? There was a first time that Jimi Hendrix picked up a guitar and he became quite good at it.

2. Use the screens for education

Watch TED talks, follow doers, watch documentaries, educate yourself. I find that all those things can serve me in a way. I become a more interesting me by taking little fragments of information from differing talks and documentaries. I can be inspired by all of these or become aware of another aspect of life that I haven't thought of before. I feel it is important for me to tune in when I watch these, I need to engage in what I watch to make it more of a learning entertaining experience than purely entertainment experience. Take notes when watching a lecture or TED talk, it engages you. Once you start learning you are on the road to becoming an expert yourself.

There is so much to learn about the world available to you. Why not use this resource that is at your fingertips? We are the first generation to have this, yet many of us choose the path of the Gilmore Girls rather than watch a lecture on evolution. We are also the first generation to have strong opinions on evolution when all the research we have done is watching Gilmore Girls.

3. Just turn it off.

Of course, there is always turning the screens off totally. Just go rock and roll style and throw the TV off the balcony. It's the mental productivity equivalent to giving up pizza and doughnuts when you want to get physically fit. It makes total sense to do that, but not to ban this unconscious, unproductive, lazy entertainment from your diet when you want to be more productive.

Cold turkey is hard at first, it requires a motivation and determination to remove it as a crutch. The hours and hours of your life that you will get back makes it totally worth it. Tell someone what you have done so you are accountable. Now stick up some goals somewhere visible and set into action the plan to get yourself away from the pretend world on the screen and into your real conscious, amazing world. Into the world of who you want to be. Within a few days, you will be thinking about the hours wasted in your life before you made this decision. The chains that had you tied to the couch are gone. You are a conscious being who isn't addicted to this thing, you are free now to do what you want.

The first thing you may notice is that you are not sure what you want to do with all this time you now have. You don't need to watch someone else's blog of their awesome day; you don't need to watch some made up drama to inject interest into your life, and you sure as shit don't need the adverts that wrap the whole experience. Make sure you have an activity planned for that time you usually would just plop on the couch and binge on screens. You need to find out who you really are and what you really can do when you have time to do it. The time that these screens are taking away from you--get outside, read, run, write, paint, create, meditate, plant, clean, laugh, talk and live with this time.

4. Plan your screen time

Try not to turn on the screen without a plan of what and how much to consume. If you don't quite feel like cutting out TV altogether then you can set yourself targets to decrease your time watching screens. You can allow yourself to watch maybe only an hour maximum a day. This is time you really feel you need after a tough day at work. Use this hour to unwind, plan what you want to watch, and only watch that. Do not switch on and look for something to watch.

If the thing you do most with your free time is watching TV and screens, I am afraid that this is your real passion. Are you happy with this if it is? You would never list watching TV or scrolling through Instagram on a résumé as one of your hobbies. You aren't proud of this passion even though it might be what you do most. It's because you know it sucks as a time consumption choice, but remember it is a choice. I know this because this was me, just randomly channel hopping watching sports, comedy, or whatever it threw at my face. Now I am aware I choose differently. You too can choose something different.

Always consciously choose to watch the screen while remembering you are not a slave to the routine of time wasting. Decide what you really want to watch and set out times at the beginning of a week when you will watch only that. The glory of YouTube and Netflix and similar is the choice and the ability to watch what you want when you want. I find joy and inspiration in what I choose to watch. I use the screen for entertainment, and I use the screen as a tool for my own goals.

The rolling from one film to another, from one episode to another, must be a decision you have already made before you started watching. I will talk about habits later in the book, but this is the habit many of us fall into so easily. Maybe it is because we have nothing else going on. This is some of us. This is a sad reality. Some people's lives resemble a machine that just works, comes home and watches screens all evening on repeat. If this resembles your life you are better than this routine. I was this routine. I was this habit. I became conscious of it and took some time to think about how I could change this aspect of my life and what I would rather do with this time. Away from the unconscious habit, I focused on what I wanted and put in place a few simple strategies that cut down on my inner slob winning the battle to get on the couch and switch off for hours. I still watch YouTube and Netflix but I am aware of the extent to which I do. I am conscious of my laziness.

Ask yourself if you are watching what you want to watch or just whatever is put on the screen for you. Are you trapped? Do you slide into the nothingness of screens while in your hand is your phone? Be aware of this, if it is what you are doing, and have a talk with yourself. Put up some goals over the TV screen or somewhere very visible when you are watching the screen. These are things you would like to achieve; these are things that your screen watching is taking away from you. I know how much you love reruns of 'How I Met Your Mother" but it's horseshit.

The time you get when you abandon the warmth and easy bullshit life of the screen is amazing. You then can say I am being me and I am doing something. I am weaving the tapestry of my life. My kids will look at their Dad and say, "Wow, how the hell did you manage all those achievements, my wonderful and amazing Father?" and I would reply "Well, son or daughter child, I turned off the screen--the shiny thing was stealing my precious time, limiting my creativity, and turning me into a drone, another number, another waste of a life".

"That's some heavy shit Father, can we watch SpongeBob?" and I would reply "SpongeBob can go fuck off," and proceed to hurl the TV off the roof of my house. You know the normal Father-Child chat.

A bit extreme, but no 90-year-old on their death bed

will say, "Man I am glad I got to see the whole series of Rick and Morty". Although it truly is an amazing show and I have watched it all with no regrets. So, I really should have said the whole series of The Sopranos for the third time was something I probably didn't need to do, and yes, I do regret wasting the time. Yes of course TV and all its equivalents can be really entertaining, and humans love to be entertained, but you need to be conscious of the true satisfaction it is taking away from your life. It is eating into your time to be here now.

What will it be? Will it be the challenge or will it be another day, week, month, year of you siting on your ass and watching other people live a life? Watching stories that someone else made up? Watching paid humans pretend to be upset about a pretend relationship in a pretend restaurant while pretending to eat with a friend who pretends to care while a pretend waiter (who isn't paid as much because he isn't as good at pretending) takes a pretend order off someone who is pretending to speak? You follow? The screen land is a getaway, yes, but be aware it is getting you away from who you could be. It stifles you. You are unique. Discover why and how to be the best you by maybe just turning the fucking screen to black.

3 YOU VS SOCIAL MEDIA

"It's fucked up how people get judged for being real, and how people get loved for being fake" Tupac Shakur.

This quote is from a man in an era before the social media world. It doesn't take much of a journey through Instagram to find pages where the love and the likes are strong for someone who is 'fake'. I suppose the question is, what is real and what is fake on social media? Is when someone uses a filter on their photos a fake? Is a person who only puts up flattering photos of themselves a fake? Is a person who isn't putting up negative aspects of their life a fake? But why would you put up negatives, who wants to remember that? Instagram is a collection of highlights. A problem with all social media is epitomized by Facebook where we are inundated with bullshit. From a statistics point of view, 86% of what you witness on Facebook is complete and utter dross. That's statistics so you can't argue with it. Fact.

Deep inside we have a 'fakometer' which can see when someone is posting bullshit. To define fakeness is difficult. People can be themselves and earn money from YouTube and Instagram and are 'real'. There is no problem with people using social media for just memories or documenting their days. Even if they aren't being true to themselves in your opinion, that really doesn't matter, does it? Be conscious that they are doing it for themselves. The issue is that many of us scroll through or watch this during our free time. This is precious time.

I wonder sometimes, do people only post to impress others? Is it healthy to constantly be putting photos of your 'best life'? Does one find pressure to be constantly in that mode? Something to be conscious of when posting: what are the reasons behind the posts you put out to the world? Can't someone just be somewhere without having to take out the phone and record it? You can't. It's just a physical impossibility. Go to a concert these days and not take out your phone and record when all your favorite songs come up. Then put them on your Instagram story. What is the point of it? Really, you miss the true enjoyment of the song just to make others jealous? The mind boggles.

There loads of influencers that have positive influence on people, changing their lives and not just a positive influence on their own bank balance. It is the way a lot of people get information daily--through pages, pictures and videos on these sites. Is it the right way? There is no right way, surely. We aren't expected to all go back to the 50's and read the encyclopedia when we don't know what an emu looks like or get the New York Times off the man in the cart to get the score of the Knicks game. Therefore, social media is important as we are updated quickly, we can be inspired by some, and we can learn from others.

Social media is a part of the modern laziness addiction, it is just so damn convenient and engaging. My strategy is for me to use it and not let it use me by following the 6 strategies listed later in the chapter.

Two stories from a yoga retreat I attended several years ago come to mind when it comes to fakeness and social media. During this enjoyable and inspirational retreat, I was amazed by two things that happened for the Instagram moment instead of the actual benefit of the real-life people there. The first one was during a silent meditation walk through a forest--wow, pretty hipster stuff, I know.

The two-hour silent walk is approximately 30 minutes from ending, our leader the yoga teacher, saw something that caught her eye--a wonderfully striking rock covered in ivy. She pointed and gestured that it was something of beauty to appreciate, which it was. She then broke rule one that she herself made and spoke, asking her colleague to take a photo of her doing a handstand with it as background. Not just taking one photo but breaking everyone's experience of silent meditation to take several until she was happy with the outcome, all the while, of course, speaking. Yup--silent meditation walk was on hold for this.

The outcome of this, of course, was an amazing handstand photo that was uploaded to 'the gram' as soon as we made it back to glorious Wi-Fi, with a description of how magical the walk was. What a crock of shit; the walk was magical until the moment a photo was required just so she could get the Instagram memory instead of the actual memory. Some feel that an Instagram memory is more important than the actual memory. The need for mindfulness about where you are when you take the photo is desperately required. How many times do you see the Instagram photo being snapped and then the "OK, let's get the fuck out of here" follow-up? Live the memories and look back and smile. Don't miss the memory for the perfect angle.

The second incident on this yoga retreat was the incident of the free interpretive dance. "Let your body go free," she said. "Move with the music as if no one here is watching". Not everyone's cup of tea, and certainly not mine, but I am up for trying most things once and this was one of those things. What's the problem with that? The problem was when two of my lovely yoga colleagues decided that they would video it for posting on social media later. Free interpretive dance is not my thing, but the whole idea of letting yourself go like no one is watching is fine when you know that you can trust everyone in the room to engage in their own experience but not when you cannot trust what the world might make of your comical timing and random movements forever. The permanence of the video alarmed me--this would be posted after on social media as to what end? Once again, the experience did not happen in these people's minds without the evidence of it on social media.

The need of the world to document everything that has happened to it and post it is becoming a must. Every moment of some people's lives, no matter how mundane or private it should be, is documented. Once it is documented, it can be stored, and stored forever. The need to impress others with your life and daily routines is incessant. You should be conscious about this; Are you doing these things for yourself? Do not do these things because someone else does. If you need memories, take photos, but save them for yourself. Why the constant need for the approval of others for what you do? Dance like no one is watching is becoming a false statement in the world of, "look, that guy is dancing, let's record it and post it" because something is happening that is slightly out of the norm.

Unfortunately, it is getting a peek into these perfect influencers' lives that we can find so interesting. We are voyeurs in a way. If someone is beautiful, rich, successful, and has a camera, we want to watch them. We watch their carefully constructed fake diary of their day. We lap it up as real. Why can't I have a life like that? As you waste your life watching someone else's life develop into a success. This should only do one thing and that is inspire you to turn off the social media and put the time and effort into the things that will make you successful and inspirational to others.

Unfortunately, we are caught in the cycle, we want to see what they achieved today, we are hooked. If it is YouTube, they have usually done something with their day, filmed it, edited it, and posted it. They are not the problem here; the influencer has been a productive person with their day. You watching their antics for the 726th day in a row is the problem here. If this is happening, they are not influencing you to do fuck all-- they are only influencing you to sit on your ass and watch them, and hopefully buy some product that has a link in the description with a 15% discount code.

Do not confuse an influencer with an inspirer. I suppose you could say one is the fake while the other is real. I find that people who inspire me don't give a fuck what I think about them. Going back to Tupac's quote to begin this section, they are real and are not putting forward some bullshit account of their polished day on YouTube.

In the world of social media, we live in a bubble created by the choices we have made in content.

24

Algorithms are used by the social media apps to map out what we 'want' to see, to keep us in a lazy loop. So, if you like watching workout pages on Instagram you are hit with advertisements for workout equipment and suggested pages to visit are workout pages. You are now in the workout bubble. It's hard to escape--it would take a major conscious effort to branch out and find new and unique content to view. Most people's time on social media is in an unconscious daze, watching and scrolling as Instagram, Facebook or Twitter decide the order and content. Are you conscious or unconscious when you scroll? The power that these companies have over what we see is immense, hence why social media influencers can earn so much money. They make it their business to sit in the center of the bubble, constantly creating content, and we will watch them as they pop up on our screen and be unavoidably influenced.

It's amazing and slightly scary. You say, "I was just talking about guitar lessons yesterday with Paul and next thing I see is an advertisement for guitar school on YouTube". How on earth did they know about my half-assed wish to become a cool sexy guitar player? How on earth indeed. Your information is not safe--anything you put on a form or search for on the internet is shared. Agencies and companies pay millions for access to this personal information. You get cold calls, cold texts, cold emails, and cold adverts every day. New ones pop up and you haven't a clue how they got your phone number. I am always interested in who replies to these messages and how the company can make enough money to make it worthwhile. All these things keep us in a bubble, a materialistic, influenced, claustrophobic, and unconscious bubble.

You can imagine yourself fighting like Jim Carey in the

Truman Show to get out of your world or your bubble in this case, noticing everything isn't quite right. It is too much of a coincidence that I am getting all these targeted advertisements, but it is the bubble we have signed up for. We didn't read any of the fine print of the terms and conditions. I know--who has the time? We get these apps for free so why shouldn't they earn their money somehow? It is totally on us to get out of the bubble, no use blaming a major company because you really enjoy their product, you know the social media dangers. You limit your intake of soft drinks because you know the damage they do to your body. Now could be the time to limit your intake of social media for the sake of your mind.

Your mind needs to grow outside of your bubble. In your stance on world issues and politics you are pigeonholed. Or maybe you don't have a stance because it doesn't affect you. You become entrenched into a position because the pages you follow, the news you watch, and content you flick through is all tailored to your view. Which way is right? After you first decided based on a young and possibly uninformed opinion on a matter, you don't get to decide anymore; you have made an absolute decision. You are for and against these things for life, because you get trapped in the bubble. Your decision rolls down the hill, gathering momentum through constant content that agrees with it. If you are for the global warming theory, you are constantly listening to opinion and content that agrees with your stance. Your opinion becomes absolute. Anyone you see on television who agrees with you 'makes valid points'. Anyone who doesn't 'is an idiot who needs to open their eyes'.

The question must be asked to yourself--are any of your viewpoints wrong? You can't genuinely think that every view you have on every issue gives you the moral high ground. In other words, are you are right in every situation? Maybe your bubble is 'protecting' you from a more informed opinion, preventing you from getting all the information and both sides of every story. Some say a true intellect will leave a discussion with a changed view to that they enter with because they are open to learning and humble enough to take on board another's point. Even if they still disagree, they might slightly change a part of their own opinion, because opinion is just that, an opinion. Are you able to change your opinion?

World issues and politics are not like football or basketball teams, you shouldn't treat them like you picked a sports team when you are five because your father supported them and therefore you are now a Lakers fan for life even though you now live in Milwaukee. Did you choose your political leaning or were you conditioned by your parents' bubble growing up? Did you choose any leaning in total independence? After you have made a decision like this, have you unconsciously followed the same path for life like a football team or for each election, each referendum, each policy, and political decision, or have you consciously informed yourself and made your own decision based on your reading and research? Maybe it is time to reset your leanings to zero and judge again from scratch where you stand on issues. That could take a while. Who has the time for that?

Time is a key throughout this book--your time is limited your time is precious and how you spend it defines you. Now think of the time you have spent on social media that does not serve a better you. The addiction is real, and you know it. You have seen the videos about it, probably on social media ironically. The screen is stealing your most valuable asset and to what end? The outcome of spending 2 hours scrolling through feed after feed should be like the feeling after you have hit the fast food outlet instead of eating a salad -- gross.

You, instead of using your time productively, have chosen to take the easy option and the quick lazy dopamine hit of the unconscious mind, the 'see what everyone else is doing' fiesta. You should be aware of it, the trap and the negativity, but you do not act, why? The triggers that social media giants have worked on and honed for years to keep you looking at the screen are working. You have succumbed to the endless scroll, the bottomless search for nothing when you pick up the phone. Why have you picked it up? It generally is not for a specific reason other than you always do it. Now is the time to make it a conscious decision.

The unconscious you wants to slip into the lazy, easy habits but the conscious you is fighting to remain productive. It directly relates to you becoming a better you; the time spent on your feeds is inversely proportional to your productivity. If you like social media, you don't have to quit it, the same way as you don't have to quit fast food if you like that. But if you want to stay in good shape you must sacrifice some of your love for delicious doughnuts and French fries. You know you can have doughnuts after you have completed a marathon, you know you can have a burger after you finish a CrossFit session, and you know you can have ice-cream after the 10k hike up the mountain. Why then do you not know you can have a little social media only after you have been productive with your mind first? Do not switch off your mind before you have used it.

Which leads me to the 6 ways to make your social media habit work better for you

1. Reward social media.

So, the solution to your social media habit may be the same solution as for someone who has a sweet tooth: Earn it. Earn the reward of the lazy dopamine scroll through the Instagram feed. Use your goals and routines, as mentioned earlier in the book, to facilitate this. You are only allowed use social media once you have painted that picture, designed that website, written that song, researched for that paper, completed that crossword, or read that chapter. Use the same methods as you would for a fitness regime. Your brain is a muscle, it needs the stimulation and the practice of mental challenge in order to grow and become more powerful. Don't let your brain turn into mush just because you are addicted unconsciously. Be conscious about this addiction and do something

2. Time social media.

The simple methods sometimes are the best. If you insist on needing the social media fix daily, set aside a certain amount of time (less than an hour) to use your phone for said purposes. You can get apps on your phone to keep track of this. Scroll away on your phone but only for the set amount of time that you have made the promise to yourself for. Another strategy for this is to have a cutoff point every evening. I would recommend at least 2 hours before you intend to go off to bed. Nothing new here again, I am sure you have heard of the dangers of screens affecting your sleep pattern. In general, just be conscious of the time you spend and be conscious whether this is good for you or not. Don't unconsciously waste your precious time. I would recommend having an accountability buddy for this, if you live with someone especially. Discuss rules you would like to implement on the amount of time spent on social media, agree to set of rules, and then help each other succeed.

3. Cleanse your social media.

Aka keep it real. The cleanse is very simple: be aware of your voyeuristic tendencies and of the voyeur ways of others. You are unique so don't imitate anyone else. You see others put up inspirational quotes, pictures by the sea, and post gym selfies, so you do the same, do it for the gram. Who are you doing this for? Are you trying to prove to other people that your life is great? Do you need their approval to feel better about yourself? Are you letting your ego take over from who you truly are? You need the comment underneath your photo about how good you look and how jealous someone else is of where you are? If you are somewhere amazing like you say, enjoy it. If you go to the gym, do it for yourself only. If you finished a book, well done, go read another. If you see an amazing quote, live it instead of sharing. And most of all, if you need to share things with people, share your amazing stories in person, share your inspiration in person. Share your thoughts in person, not a digital platform.

4. Specific numbers.

You follow so many people on Instagram, Facebook, and Twitter. You constantly scroll and are constantly hit with new content from your large number of followed people, pages, societies, news outlets, sports outlets, funny memes, funny videos, music, and other random crazy shit you like. Now is the time to limit what and who you follow to a manageable number and the things you follow. Think about how what you follow reflects on your thoughts and actions. Think about how you are in the bubble you create for yourself.

If I follow people who depress me when I see all the amazing stuff they do and how easy it is for them, how does this help me in life? Maybe I strive for what they have but it wasn't spending mindless hours on social media every day that got them there. Limit who you follow to a specific number of friends, maybe 25 to 50, 5 news outlets, 5 people that inspire you to be better and 5 pages that entertain you (sports, funny ones, music, etc.). Think also about the shit you must wade through (Andy Duphran in style) to get to the odd nugget of worthwhile information. Audit it down, forensic accountant that shit. Is it worth it? If you want to add one to the list, you must remove one as you do it. For the friends, I am sure you follow people that you do not know anymore, and you do not contact, and you are just a voyeur of their lives because let's face it, you are nosey. We are curious folk us humans, always wanting to see what others are doing, but to what end? You are satisfying a curiosity you didn't know you had in the first place. Sophie just had a baby. If you knew Sophie well enough that shit would not come as a surprise to you. Sophie and her new baby have got to go from your feed. Goodbye.

5. Be aware of your ego.

You don't need the likes. You don't need it. It's a fake situation. People are in the habit of forced liking. Ah that's Sophie--I will automatically like her picture of a cat (even though I didn't 'like' or enjoy the photo in any way) because the time will come when my ego needs a boost and I will need the like for my holiday snap riding a horse in the west of Ireland. The like for a like culture is such bullshit. What is it all about? It's about peer pressure, it's about gathering a fake group of people to boost your ego. Remove yourself from the need for a 'like'. It's not real; if you showed the person the photo on the street, they would think you a freak. Don't cave. Your intellect is stronger than your ego.

6. Turn off your social media

Remove the apps from your phone. The simplest solution of all is usually the best one.

Follow inspirational people. People who ironically inspire you not to scroll through an Instagram, Facebook or Twitter feeds. Get workout tips from those not selling anything, get inspirational quotes if that's your thing, and get motivated by people who are doing, not people who fake it. On Twitter, use that as your news feed. Search for independent news on Twitter, get a balanced opinion on world events, probably by avoiding mainstream American media. Read articles linked off there, become an informed decision maker, become an interesting person.

The most important point of all is the conscious realization that social media is stopping you from pursuing life. I can't imagine that anyone's ideal life is to mind-numbingly scroll on a phone for hours on end. Major passions or minor hobbies that get placed on the back burner by social media will fade away. Think of your life achievements as a book already written but for every hour spent scrolling, the document is slowing erasing the words. Less and less is being achieved while more is being scrolled. These achievements will be lost; you don't feel yourself losing them because they never existed, but you are losing them. This is known as "opportunity lost".

4 FAME, I WANT TO LIVE FOR EVER

Let us break down a fictional series into its basic components: someone made up a story and wrote it down, then someone got paid money to tell other people to pretend it out, then the pretenders are lauded around the world because they are good at pretending, and we watch hours of the pretending while pretending this is a great way to live. We watch the made-up stories with people pretending to fight, love, cry, and laugh for hours and hours. We are watching nonsense really. I agree it is entertaining to watch the pretending, but I feel a sense of perspective as to the importance of the pretending and pretenders is required. Society lauds these pretenders and we invest a lot of our time in this pretend world, I am not sure why.

I have spent too much time buying into the celebrity world. The book is about developing into a more conscious, less lazy human. The emphasis we put on celebrity importance over our own importance is a symptom of an unconscious human. Do you unconsciously admire someone that really you know nothing about other than they are an attractive human who happens to be good at acting? Actors are, for the most part, people wishing to be famous. An actor who is not famous is described as struggling. Every actor wants to be seen by millions and has bought into the contract that with this will come fame. This is of course a very cynical view of acting as it is a difficult craft to master, just ask Vin Diesel. It may be an unfortunate by-product of wanting to be a great actor but maybe the fame is what drives the industry as much as the art. Which came first the actor or the crowd?

They are so recognizable from the screens we watch and therefore become humans that we admire. This admiration is what needs to be reconsidered and what we need to be conscious of. These are the people that are asked for opinions on political elections and referendums. Celebrity status lends an instant gravitas to what anyone says, hence why so many of us chase celebrity--to be heard. To place such weight behind an actor's opinions and actions is an insanity of society. Are we conscious of this? The United States holds so much respect for celebrity that they elected one as their president; the guy who holds the key to the world's largest nuclear armory in the palm of his tiny hand is there because he had a successful TV show.

Seeing fame and celebrity as your overall goal in life is a dangerous quest. It leads to the saying 'be careful what you wish for'. You wish to become the celebrity that makes these YouTube vlogs? Or the famous actor who stars in the Netflix special? What would that mean your life would become? Would it be a better life? Remember, if you were famous, you would still be you, your day to day thoughts would be similar, and you probably would have all the same insecurities. Instead of a private life, you would now be constantly in the public eye, your every move stalked and criticized. No more anonymously wandering to the shops for a browse or wearing 'whatever' as you stumbled out for weekend breakfast. You would become a selfie machine, spending most of your time out of your house meeting fans and taking pictures. You could complain that you just wanted to go for a nice walk with your sister and 'no photos please' but that would mean you were now a dick for refusing a photo. This is celebrity. This is fame.

I am not sure 'famous' is ever the answer to a life goal question. In a sense it is a lazy answer to a very difficult question. Being famous should probably be a byproduct of success in a craft, but too often it comes as a result of being obnoxious. Anyway, let them have it, does fame bring happiness? A conscious human may realize that their life is infinitely better without fame. If you delve into what your daily like would be like with fame, it would be almost unbearable to leave the house. The constant harassment and staring would leave every minute uncomfortable to the non-extrovert. Could the quest for fame just be covering up for something else that is missing in someone's life? Maybe they are lonely, maybe they don't feel their work brings satisfaction, maybe they feel unheard, maybe they feel unimportant, or that their life lacks purpose. When people go home and bury themselves in the screen, they see people they think they want to be. People with purpose and social importance. The conscious mind is aware of the dangers and trappings of fame and will not pursue them for fame's sake. The unconscious lazy mind will see it as an answer to the meaning of your life.

Wealth is sometimes, but not always, a byproduct of fame. Maybe it is just wealth some people are after when they seek fame. Maybe fame is seen as the quick and easy route to a big pile of cash. Wealth has been proven up to a point as bringing increased happiness, but only up to a point where you have a comfortable standard of living. Once you reach that point then extra wealth doesn't bring the extra happiness some think it might. Realizing when you are comfortable enough and happy enough to stop striving for more wealth is where a conscious mind needs to kick in. This goes against The American Dream. There is no end to the supercars, jet skis, and indoor pools you can buy to chase happiness. Maybe keep on chasing more wealth, don't take a second to stop and enjoy what you have. Your medium sized car and house are pathetic--you need to work your ass off for 6 extra bedrooms and a sports car. If you haven't read that previous sentence in a sarcastic tone, go back and re-read in said tone. Give yourself a breath, think about what person you will be when you have these things, will you ever be satisfied? Will all the money bring you satisfaction and wellbeing?

Back to fame. If someone just says they want to be famous but not specify for what they want to be famous for, that is a problem. The problem may lie in current society's views on celebrity. They put so much weight behind celebrity opinion. Celebrities are heard and respected more than doctors, professors and accountants. But some celebrities are literally famous for being famous and are still heard. Maybe that's why so many wish to be famous, to be heard. How much weight do you put behind a celebrity's opinion? There could be an idiot celebrity on your screen telling you how to improve your sex life or lose weight, but some believe them because they are a celebrity on a screen. The latest workout video released around, hmmmm, January time, with Celebrity X revealing her secret 14-day plan to lose 27lbs. That will obviously lead to a long-term strategy to improve your health. If it's not a celebrity I am not buying it. She could have all the degrees in nutrition, science, physiology and fitness but unless she has been snapped in a bikini on the front of National Enquirer, I am not buying it, Susan.

I do realize the irony here of me giving preachy advice and comments throughout this book but be conscious about it-- only use the book to get you thinking. Just be a participant in your decisions and what those decisions mean for your life before you make them. Don't be influenced by celebrity and the famous, be influenced by your consciousness. By being conscious you also will be aware that difficult decisions must be made because the unconscious laziness may direct you down a path that is a frighteningly futile waste of your life.

To sum up the quest for fame, it is a bit like potential which we will discuss later, once you reach it, what then? OK, now you are famous for doing something, what now in your life? What does your everyday life look like? Maybe your newfound fame will open a few doors and make it easier to make money. You can endorse a few products on Instagram. Your life satisfaction and sense of purpose will not increase with this fame, even with the extra wealth. You will still be you; you won't be able to escape the inside of your head.

The glamorous ideal you imagine with fame will not be true, especially if you get to it by the cheap method. The cheap method is the instant celebrity, the overnight sensation, the reality star, the 15 minutes. You know that this is unsustainable and if you do achieve this then the rest of your life when you want to go back to anonymity will be tainted. You will be forever the girl who was on TV. If you aren't that person anymore, the public won't care, they will only know you as that 15 minutes forever.

That is a like a cheap tattoo that can't be removed. A palimpsest of regret.

The opposite to the cheap method is the craft method. The craft method to fame is deployed by those who are famous because they wanted to be the best at their craft and not because of they seek the trappings of fame. You see chefs that are famous. Presumably, they first loved making food and are only on TV because they have reached the top of their craft. These are the famous to admire and be consciously inspired by. This is not an excuse to endless watch them on TV as mentioned already in chapter 1. Build your own crafts, not for the fame but for the joy in creating. For the joy of being anonymous brilliant in the worldly scheme of things.

Isn't it great to be anonymous? Being anonymous means, you can make mistakes and try new things without fear of failures haunting you. We all know when the famous fail--the media will not let them forget. Twitter storms will come their way followed by Facebook outrage and Instagram ridicule. Find satisfaction in your current status, if it's the wealthy lifestyle you're after, find a different way. The life of fame is not a happy one. The hounding and pursuit of the famous is not worth the social status and money. Take comfort from the fact when you go running in the park no one gives a fuck. When Jennifer Aniston does it, she gets photographed. Every photo then gets analyzed, looking for imperfections. Strangers, by the million, will look at Ms. Aniston's running photos and scrutinize. She will probably just stay at home next time; the park that is open to you is closed to her.

Live life free and anonymous to strangers, appreciate what you have, think twice about emulating the famous.

5 EMPTY TIME

Empty time is the time where you are confined in your choices of space. Examples include: on an airplane, grocery shopping, traveling to work, or waiting at the doctors. This time is often where laziness is the obvious choice. However, this time is useable. It is the perfect time to improve you. It is the perfect time to reflect. With some self-talk, you could write your thoughts down in your notebook or record some audio notes on your phone. This is the time to discuss with yourself how your life is going. I find during this empty time, my self-talk leads to ideas (some amazing and some rubbish) or it can clarify what I am thinking. I give my mind time to process what is about to occur or what has just happened. Self-talk is that conversation you have in your head where you can think about your situations, decisions, plans, goals, and ideas.

I come up with some ideas when I just give my brain

time to breathe. You don't need structured meditation during empty time that, once again, is filling your time and is used to calm the mind. The true beauty of empty time is self-talk. You can motivate and create during this space you have given your mind to wander. The danger of the time is the drift into overthinking, moving away from positive creativity into the 'what has gone wrong?' and 'what will happen if something goes wrong?' thinking. Easy to say, dismiss this, and dismissing this is far easier during daytime empty time than nighttime empty time, which I will deal with later in chapter 7.

Empty time on long drives can be filled with genuine appreciation for nature while you drive. Most long drives will have something to be amazed by. Empty time in a café waiting for someone to arrive can be used to create ideas for your next move in making a better you, planning workouts in your head, visualizing your success in your next venture, running through what you want to talk to your friend about, focusing on those you are grateful for, and creating goals. Nothing needs to be, but something could be written down during this time. Embrace the ideas and thoughts in your head, get used to training your brain to focus during these times, controlling the mind into a deeply thoughtful state.

A temptation in restaurants or any situation when you are waiting is to reach for the phone, or --damn it, you left it in the car--reach for a terrible gossip magazine or even the dentist's flossing booklet. Anything to get out of your own head so you don't have to listen to your self-talk. sit, get comfortable, close your eyes if you must, and start with imagining someone you are grateful for--picture the person, send them gratitude, then move on to what you are planning this weekend. Let's think of something outside the box to do, and so on. Inability to use these opportunities is a sign of a lazy mind. You rarely get this time, so use it to your advantage. Decreased external stimulation will lead to increased internal stimulation if you choose to use, or, of course, you could just read the benefits of flossing every 38 seconds to avoid having to go back to the fucking dentist again.

The temptation with empty time is that, if you are not prepared to use it, it can take you by surprise and you fall into the radio advertisement's or gossip magazine's worthless bullshit. It is an opportunity to almost Vipassana it, speak to no one, switch off and think on what is going on in your life. Remember the choice is yours of what you do with your time. You can make the most of it of it, so make the most of it.

Some simple things you can do if you are prepared for the empty time and would rather not listen to your own head is to listen to what interests you. You can stroll around the supermarket to the sweet sounds of Jimi Hendrix, Mozart, Jay Z, Beyoncé or The Beatles. One of the great joys of life is music. You probably have style you love, and you should listen to it whenever you damn well like. Maybe if you fancy it, go on voyages into new interesting music on your Spotify or whatever. Without a doubt, trawling through multiple new bands and songs in search of gems is not always a pleasurable experience. What is new is not always wonderful, but you never know what might happen. But music is a great way to fill empty time if you are in that mood.

Music is a medium of the emotions, it can suit every mood and feeling. Listen to those classics that make you mouth the words on the subway like a raving lunatic, I am happy because '99 red balloons' is my jam. Embrace the joy it brings you; it reverberates through your soul and it can lift your mood. Use the technology available to you to create your favorite playlists for your different moods, the background of jazz when having a coffee, pump up tunes before you head out on the town, heavy metal when you work out, rap when you're feeling low, whatever it is, it is just a spice of life that is worth putting into every day. Music is just amazing. However, something that is not amazing and fills your ears with a special uber sweet sludge, is morning radio.

I used to tolerate the bullshit that fed my ears and destroyed my soul on the way to work every morning. 90% of Americans listen to radio at least once a week. Everyone knows the morning drill: host DJ and other host DJ banter runs throughout. Host to host banter, where do you start with this? It must be safe for the kids, the grandmother, and the religious alike, they cannot be offended. Rule number two, it must be upbeat and full of laughs and jokes. I say laughs, I do of course mean the fakest cringeworthy laughs known to man. I mean, what they just said wasn't funny, why is it acceptable to feed us this fakery?

Then it is the 'tease some gossip' about some minor celebrity to come after the break. The celebrity gossip tease, man oh man, the radio version of click bait: so did you hear about Miley Cyrus's latest party incident? Guess who is coming to Las Vegas next April? You will never guess who ate a hamburger yesterday? Ah listen, I don't care but something about me does care. Why do I care? Is it the air of anticipation? I don't know but you devious soul, you got me, and yes of course – it is coming up after this break. I will get to the break in a minute. Ok, Mr. Host DJ Man, I stayed through the break, tell me, inject the celebrity gossip juice directly to my veins and let me lie back in a gossip-induced ecstasy. I have fallen for it again. Mr. Host man, you got me; the gossip has concluded with a non-story about a person I never met but heard one of their auto tune one hit wonder songs. The Auto Tune One has been seen eating a burger like the rest of us mere mortals at 'In and Out' Burger. Oh my god, set my emoji to surprised cat face.

How is this serving you? Is the radio DJ a friend you need as you drive every day, a familiar voice to soothe your morning? If it is, then you be you, listen and enjoy. Just be conscious about it. The songs that are played are ones that have been proved by statistics to keep you listening. The stories that are started before the advert break are the clickbait to make you listen to the ads. The competition that is run is an advertisement for a concert, not an amazing prize for the listeners. The whole medium of morning radio has become a gateway for companies and events to plant morning seeds in your brain for the day. Seeds that will grow into ways of you parting with your hard-earned cash that you are about to make working that day. Consumer radio is trying to get you to spend your money on the way to making your money.

Americans daily are exposed to between 4,000 and 10,000 adverts a day. Surely this is some form of typo, but no. If, let's say, we give each advert one second of our time, and we choose the lower end of the scale at 5000, we would be consuming over an hour and a half of advertisements every day. Remember this is just a one second thought for each one we are exposed to. Welcome to the world of hyper commercialism, everyone. Advertising, by its nature, preys on the unconscious mind, hoping you aren't really paying that much attention and just letting ideas enter your mind as they drift in one ear and out the other. More on this later in the book.

The subconscious mind makes the choices while you mindlessly listen. Make your decisions conscious, so if you want to listen, go ahead and listen, but do it consciously by being aware of the tricks. If you plan a little bit you avoid the laziness trap. If you don't want to listen but still do because there is no alternate, let your eyes be opened to the wonderful world of audiobooks, podcasts, silence, conversations, and audio notes.

The time is here, you're trapped in a car on that run of the mill drive to work. I get it, the DJ is what you have always done. It's comforting, it's a norm. But fuck the norm. You aren't the normal, you are about the best you. The time your brain can function at its best capacity is now. You are getting older, you are losing braincells. Those of us who listen to morning radio are losing at least twice as many braincells as those who repeatedly bang their head against a concrete wall. That, my friend, is a fact.

The news comes on the radio--the world of biased and simplified stories. No, don't switch the station looking for some music. Maybe we should fill our empty time with news radio and podcasts. Being informed on what is happening in the world is a choice you can make. I can also recommend Twitter for this; follow then the reputable journalists and news stations. Unfortunately, finding your reputable sources, who are unbiased, free from any propaganda and that do not simplify events, is extremely difficult. It is not even that the news station you are listening to means in anyway to be biased, it is just receiving biased news in the first place. I am not referring to a conspiracy theory, just that humans by nature put biased spins on any story.

You have just had an argument with your work colleague. You immediately go to another work colleague friend and say your version of events which with a little bias on your part is slightly different than what occurred, making yourself out to be more in the right. We are naive to think that on a large scale, with news stories, that this doesn't happen. Get out your salt cellar because you are going to need to put a pinch in almost every story you hear, especially if it involves a press conference or a statement. Pre-planned statements are by their very nature trying to make the person, company or country making the statement look in their best light. A bit like when you go and tell Susan in Accounts about the argument you just had with the insufferable Sarah. You have biased the telling in your favor. On a larger scale, when this bias is put in place, we end up hating things we have no reasons to hate. Many of us now have hugely negative views of certain countries because of where we get our news from, we are under-informed but over-opinionated. Yes, listen to the news channels as they are useful in keeping up with world events. Don't be lazy when forming your opinions. However, I find there are many other options to use your empty time that you may want to explore.

There are so many options to improve that morning drive (and all drives). To improve the walk around the supermarket to challenge your brain to learn, to grow to be an interesting brain that others would like to have brain conversation with. Firstly, relate it to your other goals. If your goals require time for thoughts, note taking, planning or specific learning, this is the time.

Set yourself a daily topic to take audio notes on, ramble, discuss, see what comes out of that thing that brain of yours. What are your thoughts on clickbait? Are you self-aware? What are your goals? What would you like to achieve this week? What about singing practice? What about those friends you haven't thought about in a while?

Be specific for a week, each day set a topic to discuss with yourself or maybe with the other person in the car. Some interesting topics are listed at the end of this chapter.

Find an audio book you like; I have included some of my favorite books at the end of this chapter. Stick with it. Play it at 1.25 or 1.5 speed. Get through it, learn and grow. Find something that you genuinely know will make you a better person. Don't stick it out for longer than a couple of trips if it sucks, though. If it doesn't grab you or make you interested, shut that shit down. Try another one, life is too short. You must enjoy this process. Revel in the fact that you are doing you. You are a person with a shit hot growth mindset who is becoming a lifelong learner. Hey, go you.

Podcasts, cheaper than audiobooks. It can run the risk of crossing for a short period of time onto the advertisement road, but fast forward through that. Some interesting ones out there. Go on a journey of discovery. Think about an interesting you, retell the stories and interesting facts you hear. I have included some of my current favorites at the end of this chapter. As we all know, these will never age and will always be running (sarcasm). Research and find your own just in case, for some crazy reason, times change.

Music, this is the time, use the this to discover the joys and beauty of music. In my opinion, it's one of the greatest invention of humans. The pleasure you can get while going on a music journey, discovering that 'sick sick beat' (props to Taylor Swift, she nailed that song, I will hand it to her or whoever wrote it). It's cool to like whatever you like, don't be a music snob. Don't just take the shit they shove down your ear canal on the radio as your only source because it is only played on the radio because someone has connections and it sounds exactly like all the other music. Use iTunes, Spotify or another music app if you feel adventurous. Once again, find 'you' amongst the others. The 'real you' lies somewhere beyond the reeds. Enjoy music.

The empty time you have is the time to listen to yourself and time to listen to others. Nelson Mandela told a story about his father at tribal meetings allowing everyone else to talk first before he would speak at the end. Simon Simek used this and grew this idea in one of his TED Talks where he used the example of a business where the boss would say his idea first then ask for suggestions around the table. Of course, no one would come up with an idea contradicting the boss after he had already offered his opinion. Hence the ideas of the employees were lost in the choice of order of speaking.

The modern world values speaking far more than listening. Everyone has an opinion that they must share, everyone's voice has a platform on social media where they can shout from the mountain top their valuable words. Everyone else is on their mountain top also shouting super important 'woke' stuff. The world is so interested in speaking, it's boring to listen, it's difficult to listen. We rightly ignore some of the social media shouting from the mountain peaks but often we do the same to those who are physically in front of us. Physical conversations are a skill and it is being lost to the world of non-engagement in the now. Just think of the dying art of phone conversations where you must listen intently. I avoid them too; I am improving my listening skills but the long phone conversation is still trial for me.

Others should be valued; the key to listening is not to judge before you listen to what the other is going to say. It is a lazy approach where you aren't willing to put in the effort of consciously listening. You may not value the person or what the person says before they say it. This is your ego judging people. You are a bit of a dick if you think you are above listening; when they take time to speak you switch off and shut down until they finish speaking whereupon you immediately shoot the idea down. In your opinion, you are right and that makes all your ideas better and others not worth your ear time. But if you listen, you could be wrong or could slightly change your idea for the better. At times your ego won't let you listen, but a conscious person will be there tuning in and getting something from the experience.

A good listener is a person that people want to be around. That doesn't mean you are Sigmund Freud sitting on your chair taking notes while others come to use you as a sounding boards while lying prone on your couch. It means you are mindfully engaged in conversations. You are someone who replies with meaningful followup questions, sage advice, or a contrary argument. This can be difficult to do, the lazy approach of bulldozing a conversation where you want it to go is easier. The ability to listen well keeps conversations flowing and interesting and you can gain something from each deep conversation you have where both sides listen and consider the others. Remember, conversations are not competitions to outscore the other person.

The outdoer — the person who listens only to formulate what they are going to say next. They are formulating a time where they did something more impressive or waiting to tell you how much worse their life is. This is common practice in circles that the author has been involved in. "You know I had a pretty shit day; I spilled my coffee on my leg this morning and opened my door into the parked car beside me." And now the outdoers reply, "Oh you think that's bad, I had a whole pot of coffee spilled in my lap and a car rammed into the back of me last week," only to be further outdone by another outdoer, "Oh you think that is bad, Susan? Just yesterday I had a coffee truck run me over and decapitate me." I win the story because mine is the worst.

When someone is telling you about their rough day, this is a chance to listen, empathize, and cheer someone up because they are having a rough day. You listen, you engage, and you react in a way that makes you a good human. No need to judge or find something similar in your life to compare it to, just take it at face value and listen. Some people just cannot do this, they cannot engage when listening.

The non-engaged – they wait and bide their time, inside sighing, come on come on finish what you have to say, I have this thing I want to talk about. "Ah very good, Daisy, so, I ran into Mike at the store yesterday and he said that Jeff had broken up with Madison. Do you think he would be interested in me?" We maybe have all been guilty of this, we have news or interesting gossip and this story, that you are hearing, is just boring. Be conscious of your non-engagement and try and be selfless in your responses. Maybe a good listener can be defined as the person who listens and responds without judgement and continues the conversation in a logical fashion without ego.

Some people realistically do not care about you or what you say; they have their own shit and troubles going on. They have empty time of their own, where they over-think and analyze their lives, so don't be too quick to worry about people not listening to you. You listen to you, you decide what is important to you, discuss it in your own head during your empty time, and react accordingly by setting your sights on where you want to be. Being a better listener can be a huge advantage when looking for advice.

Ask for advice on how to get to where you want to go. Do not be overwhelmed by ego whereby you do everything on your own. When you do ask, listen. Other people are experts in the experience you are going through, ask them questions on how they succeeded and got there. If you want to know anything about my experience of writing an average self-help book drop me an email on johndcollinsauthor@gmail.com. Or people have failed in the their attempts to do what you are about to set out on, for me these people, if you find the right one, are more interesting, you definitely learn more from mistakes than successes, why not learn from other's mistakes? Why do we only read books of the 1% of businesses that succeeded? Maybe because we are chasing success, but what we really need advice on is what can go wrong, not the lucky breaks and hard work of a success. So maybe you can also email me about why I am not a millionaire rock star on johndcollinsauthor@gmail.com or check out my blog at fightlaziness.com. See more on this in the Shit Happens section in chapter 14.

Top 3 audiobooks to try

1. Power of Habit – Charles Duhigg

Listen and put into place your habits. It literally could change your whole life for the better and make you more productive once you see how important and destructive habits can be. Learn from this book and then put what you have learned into practice.

2. Sapiens – Yuval Noah Harari

Mind blowing stuff which will make you question everything that we take for granted. Money only works because we all agree it works. Religion, well just listen to it and make up your own mind.

3. Can't Hurt Me – David Goggins

You want motivation, you fucking got motivation. This man will make you think about striving to be the best you can be especially from a fitness standpoint. Also, an interesting take on the Audiobook format including interviews with the man between each chapter.

Top 3 podcasts to try

1. Joe Rogan

Not everyone's cup of tea, but he gets some amazing and interesting guests. People you don't agree with are as valuable, if not more so, to the conscious mind than those you do. See what makes different people tick, almost all guests are 'successful' in a chosen field. Full of knowledge bombs.

2. Hidden Brain

Stories that open your eyes, science that sparks your brain, just good genuine listening for anyone interested in the world. Serious and lighthearted, never taking itself too seriously. I really enjoy the style of Shankar Vedantam.

3. Freakonomics

Delve into the world of socioeconomics, sounds boring but it's impossible not be interested in what they have to say, topics like Sumo wrestling, soul possession, and lottery loopholes are discussed.

Ten random questions to discuss when you're driving with someone

What would your perfect day look like?

What is your biggest regret? What is your biggest regret this week?

Who are you grateful for?

Is the supernatural just the yet to be explained natural?

Who are the 5 people in the world who inspire you?

When you look back on your life can you think of a turning point?

What has been your favorite travel experience?

What is your greatest accomplishment? What would you like it to be?

What is something you learned in the last week?

If no one existed in the world but you, how would you dress?

True Empty Time can be sought once you are comfortable with it, once you are comfortable in your own company. You can go to spaces that allow you to think. If you can be at peace with just you and your mind with no material stimulus, isn't that real happiness? Some refer to this as spirituality, others think of this as meditation or the religious, this inner peace. I don't know what to call it, but we can all achieve it. It may be the hardest thing to do sometimes, nothing, truly nothing.

Calming the mind and contemplating life, watching your anxiety and fears disappear. Maybe you come to the realization that all you need in life is to give love to others, maybe that is true spirituality and the pinnacle of using your empty time.

6 THINGS

Living my best life? What exactly is that again? Why do we move to big cities to work hard to get an unsustainable mortgage and an overpriced car? Who is to blame for this materialist race to the top? Ah, the government and big business. Nope, it's us, for buying into this rat race shit and believing advertising. There is somewhere inside us an inner magpie attracted to the bullshit shiny thing that will make our blackbird life better. It is inbuilt into a blackbird, but it is learned by a human. Is it through accumulated battering from advertisers that we succumb? We subconsciously reckon it is easier to join them than beat them. OK, I will buy the waffle maker and the Adidas top--don't forget to send the pic on Instagram. Advertising has made us look down on the used and not shiny. Good old advertising.

I used to want to work in advertising as a young man, thought it would be cool, like Mel Gibson in "What Women Want" (such a different time). I would be working for a famous shoe manufacturer trying to sell the latest overpriced Bangladeshi slave labor-produced lavishly designed trainer. Trying to sell this trainer to an over-privileged, annoying, spoilt child with some skateboard or BMX-based commercial where the kids pulled off a cool triple twist (I know nothing about either of these activities, but it sounds like it could be a thing). It ended with a clever tagline -- something to do with freedom. What complete and utter bollocks.

Watching these advertisements between or before our screen binge is part of the watching experience. We look at adverts such as Nike's more recent one, "Believe in something, even if it means sacrificing everything" with Colin Kaepernick and maybe unconsciously take nothing on board. It is a clever piece of advertising that speaks to the side of the moral high ground and the right to free speech in the United States. The cynical amongst us may see this as an attempt to line Nike up with the moral high ground. Didn't you know the high moral ground sells trainers? Is the high moral ground like this advertising campaign better than no moral ground? Does this campaign bring attention to an issue that deserves attention? The main thing that was discussed after the campaign released was not the issue of race in the United States but the effect of the advertisement on Nikes sales. Was racial prejudice was used to sell trainers? News segments and articles would mention the reason behind the campaign but then go on to show photos and videos of Nike products. These multiple mentions of Nike and stirring controversy is fantastic advertisement. Any publicity is good publicity.

Other controversial campaigns run by Nike included Lance Armstrong post drug test failing, Maria Sharapova also post drug test failing and Tiger Woods post sex scandal. The question a conscious human must ask is why a sports brand is doing this? Is it for some obligation to the people of the world to provide them with a moral compass, or is it to sell trainers? A quick search for job descriptions for marketing managers in Nike will lead to phrases like "maniacal consumer focus", "achieve budgeted business revenues" and "ensure all marketing activities deliver". This is not an attack on Nike but more a discussion on advertising in general. Nike's job description points only to money making and no mission statement on moral rights. The key point here is that Nike, like other companies, use whatever they can to shock and create controversy only to get their name in the media and hence sell more. These are marketing money making strategies. Strategies used to make us buy products and nothing else. It is our fault as consumers if we lazily lap this up. We just love buying shit.

The need for the instant hit of buying something new has led the author down the debt path of buying cars, furniture, guitars, and things. I can still remember the first guitar I bought when I was 15. I was working in a furniture shop doing the grunt work and generally being useless at most things other than making tea and running to the store. Next door to the furniture place was a music store where I first set eyes on the Burns Guitar of my dreams. A beautiful mix of black and deep rich orange. Oh man, it was sexy. But I had to have it. So much so, that I bought it at shop window price and paid it off over the next 3 months. If I had saved first and then bought it for cash it would have been 25% less. This was my first step into the world of consumerism, poor self-discipline, and debt.

I have firsthand experience of the car market taking me for an advertising sucker. About 10 years ago, I was driving the best car I ever owned--nothing exciting, a mid-ranged Ford, a few years old, but it had everything I wanted in a car. So, as any sensible and conscious decision-making human would do, I saw something shiny in a car advertisement and went for it. The new car had electric this and that, oh, and the salesman was an ex-sportsman who gave me the full charm offensive. I drove it during the test drive and even commented to the salesman, "I think it's slower than my own car." "Ah", he said, "The engine is just a bit cold." "OK." He must be correct, he knows more about cars than little old me.

I traded in my excellent older car for the modern piece of excrement. That modern piece of excrement was the bane of my next 5 years, consistently breaking down with electrical problems while I constantly paid off the loan I had taken out to buy it. I was literally paying this car dealership 500 dollars a month to drive a worse car than I had before. All because I bought into the advert, I needed the shiny thing I saw on the billboard, it was very pretty. But there is one other reason I bought the car and it shames me to say it. I caved into materialist pressure.

When purchasing any large ticket item since, I have always remembered the pain that that car purchase brought to my psyche. I bought something I didn't need and didn't really want. Why? The first reason was to keep up with my peers, who all had nicer shiny pieces of metal on wheels to get them from A to B. They would joke about my old car sounding like a tractor and that theirs were more modern. My car wasn't sexy, but I really liked it and it was perfect for me. But I caved and started to notice all the car advertisements, I must have thought the advertisements were right: I do need the new shiny thing, I do.

The second pressure I caved into was the subtle

constant advertising catching my eye with the models, the car driving in Monaco, and the sporty wheels, oh they had me. Beautiful people and places really do work on humans. It is why models have jobs. It is a no-brainer to have a sexy model beside your car when you launch it at a motor festival. In a massive shock to everyone, the male unconscious mind is attracted by the model. There are studies that show that men see women as objects when marketing is done in this way. Maybe subconsciously men are being convinced that the woman beside the car either comes with the car or the car would facilitate the gain of the woman.

The third part is, I caved to the salesman. I think, looking back, that I didn't want to disappoint the salesman after he seemed so enthusiastic, or I didn't want to seem like I wasted his time. I knew I didn't want or need to buy the car, I still ended up buying it. The biggest one-time purchase of the first 36 years of my life was made because I couldn't say no to a salesman, I couldn't take a bit of ribbing from my friends, and I couldn't resist advertising. I was not in charge of my own decision making. It wasn't laziness in this case, it was something else. The conscious me was pushed back into a dark corner of my brain. I knew it was a bad idea, in fact, I remember I lost quite a bit of sleep following the purchase knowing that I had messed up, but still I wouldn't go back tail between legs and say I changed my mind. I let my ego take over. I couldn't return it out of pride. I was, and still am, disappointed in myself and have vowed never to be that weak-minded again. I caved to materialistic pressure.

In a follow up to this, years later, I almost did it again with another car. I was ready to put a deposit down on a brand new electronic and gadget-laden 4x4 that once again, would have tied me to a long loan. I, this time, left the showroom to think, to breathe, and to analyze my options. I was very close to buying this car. Oh, it was very close, because it looked cool in the advert and the salesman had played a blinder again. This time, though, I went home, I went from 90% certain to buy when I was in the showroom to a realization that once again, I didn't need it. I ended up buying a 10-year-old, used 4x4 that lasted me 4 years with very few problems. Sure, it wasn't the newest car on the road but when it needed fixing, it was so much cheaper than my friends' repair bills and when it came to pay for in the first place, it was 20% of the price of the new model.

I put thought and effort into the purchase, I analyzed for quality, I researched the brand and issues, I looked for a car that had easy-to-find spare parts, that had a lot of similar models on the road, that had good reviews, and that I liked the look of. When I had done that thinking and research it was a no brainer. Both cars brought me from A to B. One car would have brought me into debt. The adverts, models and salesmen lost this round and will never beat me as easily again. I avoided the lazy approach and put the effort into buying.

This is where laziness costs people money. Some people think it is too much effort to research and shop around for better deals. This lack of effort is shocking when you consider how hard it is for you to earn this money. If you save a thousand dollars when buying a car by a few hours research and a few extra miles traveled wouldn't it be worth it? In the past I have been too loose and easy with my hard-earned cash. I should have learned more from my father who was far more frugal. His frugality was difficult, it came with detailed accounts of every little expense so he could afford to send his kids to college. His lack of laziness allowed myself and my siblings get a better education. I am grateful for these efforts.

Without doubt, the most first world of first world problems is having too many things. The accumulation of stuff. I currently own two L-shaped 4-man couches and one reclining chair. I have never had more than 5 people sit in my sitting room, yet I can seat 9. Why on earth do I have so much seating? Because I saw, I wanted, and I got it. Unconscious purchasing--where we buy because we have convinced ourselves of a need or that we are getting a good deal so therefore the unnecessary purchase is justified. We almost buy the deal rather than the item, just because it is good value. I bought the couch. When I did it, I justified it by the fact that I needed to fill the space in my apartment. My apartment that was too big, so I paid more for a larger apartment so I could spend more money filling it with furniture to make it look nice for the people I don't invite over.

A conscious mind would have put both those decisions through a wringer--do I need this size of an apartment currently? Will I need it in the future? Do I need to fill the space? Do I need to fill the space with the 2000-dollar couch? A good strategy for avoiding such large and unnecessary purchases is the 24-hour rule: Go to the furniture store, be taken by that amazingly comfortable couch, be charmed by that slick salesman, but then, instead of taking out the cheque book, you go home. 'I will be back tomorrow', the salesman will convince you that tomorrow the deal could be gone, you are better off taking it now. The salesman knows that impulse is on his side, a thoughtful purchaser may buy the couch, but the chances are lower because he knows you will go home and look around see you don't really need it and do the math on your bank account. You don't need it and you should save that money for what is important. Sale cancelled, tough luck, slick sales guy, pick on some other sucker.

Another major issue with things is the cost. General rule of thumb is to buy things you, after careful consideration, need. Buy a quality version of that thing. A friend of mine has a saying --and I am sure he borrowed this from someone else-- 'I am too cheap not to buy expensive shit'. I am sure you have figured this one out, but his theory is that if he needs to buy something, for instance a jacket, he will test, research, and find the best quality and most comfortable jacket. He will test and try until he finds the best one and will buy that. In almost every case, it is one of the more expensive ones he has tried. But the theory is, that if he likes it, it is quality and durable, it will last longer and be of more use than the 3 other cheaper poor-quality jackets he would have purchased. As in, he would purchase a cheap one and need to replace it three times in the timeframe he would need to replace the quality one.

This rang true to me in so many ways, especially when it comes to clothes. How many bargain shoes did I have to buy before I realized that one quality pair of shoes lasts longer, hurts my feet less, and are more stylish than 4 pairs of knock offs? Do your research, don't settle for the cheapest option, often it is a false economy. You will spend more in the long run. In essence, you are looking for value for your money. This is just another example of being a conscious decision maker. Weighing up the pros and cons of purchases, which is better? Do I need this item? Have you the ability to resist the instant gratification of the purchase? Yes, you can because you are no longer a 6-year-old child and don't need it now.

Do you have the ability to analyze a product for quality, rather than be trapped in the 'Oh look it's so cheap' loop of lazy false economy? Quality over quantity every day. When it comes to parting with your hard earned cash for products, think of the fact that you have given up your time to earn the money so be sure when you are handing it over that you treat it with the same value as you should treat your time.

The collection of things can lead to the human comfort cocoon. The warm and relaxing trinket-filled space we call home. If we are lucky enough to have a space to call our own, we generally as humans fill it with the obligatory stuff. The more stuff we accumulate the more the cocoon wraps around us. The cocoon ties us to one place and makes it difficult to move your life. It limits our ability to travel the world; we won't take the job in a new area or country because of the comfort in our current environment and because of the effort of moving our things. The amount of stuff we have enables our laziness. In the end, we choose our trinkets and TVs over experiences and opportunities. I have no doubt when we lie on our death beds that we will never take pleasure in the fact that we didn't take more opportunities in life to see the world and do shit. We didn't take the opportunities to see the world and meet new people because we were comfortable watching reruns on our couch after a tough week with all our carefully laid out knick-knacks surrounding us.

Assess your life priorities and what living is. If you are quite happy with these decisions of your living situation, then so be it. The only person to judge you is you. See that you have made a conscious decision to stay in the place you live and not an unconscious decision to be enveloped by comfort. Is the cost of buying all these things, adding to the weight that will tie you down? Moving is one of the major stresses in a human's life and is not an easy thing to do. Maybe staying in the same place is a later regret. Very difficult to balance between the two, be aware of the cocoon and be comfortable when you have made the right decisions for you.

The danger of material goods is the obvious. We all know it, they are things, they cannot and should not be a route to happiness. They lack the depth to bring anything other than an initial thrill of purchase followed by the mundane routine of using or looking at the thing. Don't get me wrong, I have things, every human has things, but as a conscious human, these things cannot fulfill me.

Remember to breathe before you buy. I mean take your sweet ass time buying, asking questions of the seller and more importantly of yourself. Have an empty time conversation with yourself on it (see chapter 4). Another safeguard is to run it by a friend, a friend who knows you and a friend who won't be afraid to tell you what's what. If they ask you "do you really need?" and you then start to over justify the purchase, then you probably don't need it. Save that cash, wait for an experience or an opportunity where you will be thankful that cash is still there and ready to be used on something more worthwhile.

The moment of happiness but long-term emptiness that things bring can become even more tragic if the purchase was made without the money in the first place. Some consumers love material goods so much they borrow money to purchase. It is incredibly common; it has happened me. Debt has a direct relationship with unhappiness and stress, yet we still will buy the new couch on our credit cards. Consumer debt at time of writing is over 4 trillion dollars. The average American household is in debt, from multiple sources with multiple figures but they all agree an average American is in debt. A recent survey has found that more than half of Americans have less than 1000 dollars in savings.

Unconsciously putting material goods too high on the priority list is an issue. I always think back to that time I purchased a car instead of 5 years' worth of experiences. I bought a car when I had a perfectly good one when I was 26, I paid it off at 31. Stupid decision, ego driven, not thought through and it brought me no happiness. Moment of pride when people saw it first and commented on how 'sweet' it was. That faded after a week. People don't give a toss then, they only said it to be polite in the first place. Their politeness probably masked the good advice they wanted to give, "What the hell was wrong with the other one?" Nothing, absolutely nothing.

Don't be that person. You are better than dumbass 26-year-old me. If you are buying something extraordinary to impress people, these are the people who are not needed in your life. Think about investing in yourself and not in a collection of stuff to impress those others.

We are a species that values things more than people. The value of a person you might think is immeasurable, but every day it is someone's job to weigh up the cost of human life. We make decisions on how safe is safe enough. Sure, we could impose speed limits of 30mph all over the world, pedestrians and car drivers would be safer and therefore cause fewer deaths. But productivity would decrease and big business would lose money so we set the speed limits higher. Instead of lower speed limits we try and make cars that will increase our survival rate as both pedestrian and driver. We know fewer people would die if we went to 30mph, but we are quite happy to allow the higher speed limits in pursuit of further monetary gain.

Not an exact price on a human head but an example of where a human life isn't quite as valuable as we may think.

We can apply this logic to workplace safety, especially in some developing nations where a human life, like it or not, is worth less money. In the most developed countries, workplace safety means a huge cost in the price of developing new buildings and infrastructure, hence a slower and more expensive rate of expansion. Unions and lawyers ensure that humans going to work in these societies are compensated for dangerous jobs and have all the necessary safety equipment and procedures. This is, as many of us would think, how it should be done, human life is so precious that it doesn't matter if it takes extra years to build the new freeway as long as safety comes first.

Now for the contrary example, now to Dubai. An area of rapid building and progress, the site of the World Expo 2020. How can they build everything so quickly, how have they managed to produce these magnificent buildings? It's the oil money, right? No, it could be the lack of value they place on certain human life. The value they place on the humans that they fly in from the lesser developed world of Bangladesh, Nepal, and Pakistan is exponentially smaller than that of their own Emirati people. This is, of course, not limited to Dubai--many countries in the world are similar but it is a problem on the building sites in the fast-expanding cities in the Middle Eastern region. The humans that work on these building sites are paid about 10 dollars a day, in the country where it is not unusual to pay 10 dollars for a cup of coffee and steaks come covered in gold. These humans work for 6 days a week, 12-hour shifts and live in 10 to a room dorm. These long shifts take place in incredible heat. Is the price of one Sri Lankan worker worth the price of building the Burj Khalifa? In Qatar so far in preparation for the 2022 FIFA World Cup, it is estimated by the Washington Post that 1200 workers have died in the construction of the stadiums and that figure is very likely to have risen significantly by time of reading.

Of course, you literally can, and people have, calculated the price of a human life. In Russia, the price is around 2 million dollars, in America, around 7 million dollars and in Australia, around 4.5 million dollars. With some quick math, the price of building the Burj Khalifa is around 2000 humans. Simplistic view of things, I know, but it makes you think. We, as humans, value things more than people.

An example of this came in April 2019 when the Notre Dame Cathedral was gutted in a huge fire. The money raised post the fire exceeded one billion dollars in a matter of days. It could have been used to save many French citizens' lives in need to medical treatment and have some left over to help all the homeless in Paris find accommodation. Some say that a human life is of immeasurable or infinite value, but we as humans consistently do not follow this view. Actions speak louder than words. How much is your life worth?

7 RELATIONSHIPS

The 'one' is hard to find. Say I am looking for a tall, dark, and handsome 26 – 39-year-old doctor who has his own house with immaculate cleaning habits, likes children, has a dog, is driven, rich, and dresses well? OK, what if you find this dream man, what if he is a right prick? What if he thinks you aren't up to his high standards? You may be hearing this for the first time but finding the right person for you can be hard. Even when you think you have found them, have you really found them? These external traits are not something you can have a conversation with. I know this is the ground-breaking content you have been expecting. This guy is breaking new boundaries, he is opening my mind, he is Captain Obvious. Water is wet FYI, just in case that one passed you by, too.

A partner is someone you plan to spend your life's journey with. The journey is not the destination of husband/wife, two kids, and a house in the suburbs. The journey is the thousands of meals you spend together, the hundreds of vacations, and the millions of words you share. They are the person that you expect to be with when you retire sitting on the front porch drinking coffee in the rocking chairs looking with disparagement at the kids of today's antics. "Back in my day, we had respect for our elders, and we played football on the street like healthy kids". I am not sure what the teenagers of today are going to say when it is their turn to sit on the fictitious porch of the elderly, 'back in my day we had good healthy pastimes like spending 4 hours a day playing Fortnite, sending duckface selfies on snapchat and scrolling endlessly through social media posts, and look at these kids today, wasting their lives'. OK, I have gone off track, but it is freaky to think what on earth will the kids of 50 years' time be doing that today we would be disgusted by? My prediction -- a total shut down of all free speech in a whirlwind of political correctness. Say nothing, you might offend.

You require a life partner, someone who you are going to spend your precious time with. Who is worthy of me? Only the imagined perfect stereotype person, who I have picked based on external features and qualities, will do. You know that this is wrong, but you still do it. For women, it seems important to have a man who matches or exceeds their own earning power and perceived job importance. For men, who knows what goes through men's heads? "Eh, she has gotta be hot, bro".

I don't know-- and no one can claim they do know-- what goes through men's and women's heads when they are eyeing up a potential partner. There is a stream of unconsciousness and consciousness that is hyper complicated and open to philosophical argument.

Knowing exactly in each person what that process looks like is impossible. I can presume it is the same for all men as it is for me, but I already know that not to be true. This is called the false consensus effect or bias. I cannot presume a consensus in all male's opinions on women or men for example, nor can I presume that there is a consensus with my specific opinion. Therefore, I am unable to say what you should look for in a partner but can give examples of what I think can help maintain a happy relationship. You decide whether it would work for you or not. What I have done is listed 5 traits that you could look for in a potential or current partner or yourself. Remember this isn't Hollywood--real life is the day to day, not the grand gestures. A little bit of effort and avoiding lazily taking each other for granted is a good place to start along with these traits.

Attitude

Attitude is important in life, in everything we do, in the way we present ourselves to others. In a relationship you must be willing to try new things and not just in the large sense. Accept and try new little things--such as, a difference in washing the dishes routines when you have just moved in together, a new bed-time or wake up time to facilitate a partner's goals, or breaking a routine to do something your partner has thought about as being fun. Approach each of these with the right attitude. Spreading negative emotions to a partner's new idea can lead to resentment. Remember any time someone shot down your new idea instantly, it didn't feel good. Smile and give it a try; if it is not working for you discuss and make changes.

Ego

You do not have to be right all the time. A difficult one for me at times. If you are wrong, admit you are wrong, not in a begrudging way, but in an honest and self-deprecating way. Everyone is wrong from time to time and if you let your ego tell you otherwise, that is bullshit. How you react to being wrong will affect how your partner reacts when they are wrong. Keep an open mind to your lack of knowledge and how you don't always know what is best. Simple things like the best route to go to the beach can become an issue that ruins the day when your wrong turn 'short cut' means you must walk for an extra half hour. How do you deal with being wrong? Take it on the chin, with grace and acceptance, lighten the mood and move on. Do not let your ego ruin experiences. When you are the right one, which those of us with the big egos always think we are, remember when proven right don't be a smug head, just don't. You may not think it, but you are wrong about half the time, remember this before your ego develops into an 'I am always right" monster.

Time

Such a huge part of a relationship. For me it is split two ways. Time with the partner and time without the partner. It is easy to become lazy about giving your time to your partner.

Time with the partner needs to be valued. Our time on the planet is finite. Time outweighs money when it comes to your life. Give time to your partner's ideas, goals and plans. Give time to listen to what they have to say. Take time to specifically eat with them for any meal you can, and do it at a table so you can talk. When you are in the car, use the empty time to turn off the radio and have a chat about something. Every minute is an opportunity in a relationship, an opportunity to grow the relationship if spent together in the right conditions. Make time for each other, use it to do things each of you like and things you both enjoy.

Time away from each other is also crucial. No one enjoys being suffocated, well I don't think so anyway, unless you're into auto-erotic asphyxiation. Your partner and you should have independent time to do independent goals, support them in this. Also, it is important to have time to meet different friends. Friendships independent of the relationship are a healthy thing that allows us to have different conversations, that maybe as a couple we are not interested in having. This time apart must be communicated well so as not to blindside either partner. Plan times in advance so no one else's plans are put out by your last second glass of wine with the girls.

Value

You must see it as an amazing thing that some other human on the planet has decided of their own free will to spend an elongated period with you. They have accepted your faults and failings and have embraced your talents and intelligence. You are both valued because you have chosen each other. Remember that, when it comes to decisions in your lives, place that value as the number one priority in the decision. Do you promote that value when people speak to you about your partner? You should. You are 'team together' in the world. Show them how much they are valued and cherished with little things.

Little things

My favorite part of relationships is the little things that are the spice of the relationship. Every so often, the little love note, the random shoulder rub, the nice thinking of you text message, the phone call out of the blue, the 'I made you coffee', 'I bought you a little trinket today', ' there is food in the fridge', a voice message to ask if you got home safe or 'I bought you flowers' --all these things bring a smile to my face. None of these things cost an extraordinary amount of money or any at all, and all take very little time and effort, but they are an amazing part of feeling valued and special in a relationship. Each one brings you warmth inside when you receive and each one should bring joy to give. Express gratitude when you receive and don't do it because you feel obliged, do it because you want to bring a smile to their face. You want to make them happy and enjoy life with you that little bit more. Do not wait for the right time, just put down the book now and do something for somebody, even if you are single, do something for your friend, partner, or sibling. Spread the love through little things.

3 conscious steps to finding the one

1. Make yourself first

A partner doesn't define you; you define you. Be ambitious and constantly improving yourself. In a way, you are making yourself a better 'catch', but that shouldn't be the goal. Not many find laziness an attractive quality. This book is about valuing yourself and the time you have on this planet. Make sure you don't waste it and that is totally up to you. Take charge of your life. If you are single and spending more time complaining about being single and scrolling through Instagram and Facebook on repeat, depressing yourself into the state of self-pity while you look at others perfect Instagram lives, you are fucking wasting your life. Get up and be a better you instantly. Get your shit together. What are your goals? As is discussed in the next chapter, get your goals, habits, ambitions and routines in place to a be an awesome you first because you value yourself before you need others to value you.

2. Value yourself

The reason you are improving yourself is because you value yourself. You can see that with this one life you have finite amount of time to achieve. Value your time and abilities. Build yourself into the awesome you. Have no doubt, the more you value yourself, the more others will start to value you. Do not give your time to those who do not give their time to you. Are they not responding to a message? Screw them. Are they treating you like the dirt on their shoe? Screw them. Are they playing hard to get? Screw them. I, of course, mean screw them very much in the non-sexual way, lol. If you are in this cycle of not finding 'the one' because you are the 'desperate one', be aware of it now. Now set out the plan to be a better you first and others will see you as the catch, but only if you aren't trying to be the catch--the reason is just for you. Once you have done that, now you can go.

3. Now go

Now go is the hardest part if you haven't done the other two steps. Most people have started on now go. Straight into the world of finding the one without finding themselves first. Hang on a minute, you want to get romantic and settle down and have kids then realize that you haven't done anything with your life and your partner is not as driven as you need. If you are an ambitious, conscious human, you need to be ambitious and driven when you meet your potential partners, otherwise don't expect them to just match your ambitions when you do eventually realize you have them.

So, you have done steps one and two, now ready, set, goooo. Put yourself into interesting groups of people without the intention of meeting anyone, just because you are now an interesting person, people will gravitate to you and find you intriguing if you've got stuff going on. Go to classes to learn new things if you are struggling to find situations where you would find interesting people. Talk to people when you are out and about, people you find attractive and interesting in the bookstore, the clothes shop, the supermarket, the gym--nothing too much, maybe just a 'hi'. You will know if they are intrigued or they aren't. You are now someone who values yourself and has a lot going on, so you should be confident enough to wait and bide your time. Going doesn't mean go to the club and get shitfaced, it means go put yourself in good situations where people who would interest the best you would be.

Just as important as your romantic relationship, are your friends. Who do you spend time with? A good friend is obviously someone who is there for you, think about your friends. Right, you are up shit creek without a paddle, your car broke down, you broke up with your partner, you messed up royally or you are just feeling shit. Who do you call? Who would and could you rely on? You surely have someone in mind? Maybe you are lucky and have more than one person. Maybe it's Paul who is a bit annoying because he won't stop droning on about basketball. But that dude you are thinking of, that's a good dude. That's someone to cherish. Go hug him. 'Hey Paul, you want a hug?'

A 'bad' friend is someone you are only there for them and not in reciprocal. Make sure that you aren't this to the aforementioned Paul. Think about whether you have been there for him or given him the cold shoulder when he asked for that ride somewhere or to borrow your hair straightener. Bad friends use you. Be conscious of those who are 'bad' friends and if you are being a 'bad' friend. Think about when you were in school or college and there was always some girl you looked up to or wanted to be their friend and they would just keep you on the edge of their circle, the slightest intersection in your Venn Diagrams. Remember they would come a running when they needed to finish their essay or needed the notes for the class they skipped. Britney is so cool, she just texted me. She is using you Madyson, using you.

Don't be that bad friend and try not to keep those bad friends in your life. Slowly fade them out, cold shoulder style. Do they contact you to see how you are? Michelle only ever messages me when she needs a lift somewhere.

There are many layers to friendships and those friendships are tough to keep ticking over nicely. You've got to put effort into friendships. Why? They require maintenance, constant checking in. Work at friendships-- they are important. That might mean being the one who sends the "How are you?" messages for no reason, just because. You sometimes just think of people, why not then contact them and tell them that? Taking friends for granted is the lazy approach.

Now you've been thinking about your friends in life, lucky you, you got some friends, congratulations. Maybe you have sorted them out into good and bad friends. You got to love the technical terms good and bad, I was a quite the wordsmith in school. A prolific user of nice, good, and fine. Anyway, getting back on track, let's look in the mirror and ask ourselves the question am I a good friend? A serious self-reflection may lead to some troubling results. Have you broken a friend's trust by letting a secret slip out that you had promised or even pinky promised not to tell? I wonder is pinky promise legally binding in a court room? I bet there has been a case brought to court. I could look it up, but I am happier in the ignorance. Have you ever ignored a minor plea for help because you had your own plans? I could give him a ride to the store, but I just wanted to go for a run after work and then vegetate on the couch. Have you ever not been honest with a friend for whatever reason, to save face or even to save their face? Maybe it was just to avoid conflict? Is this then a healthy friendship? There is one thing that makes you or anyone a good friend. Giving time.

Time is the currency of the conscious human. You must value it as your most precious commodity--you just don't know how long you have here on the earth. So, if you are truly a friend, you will spend time with that person. If you are too busy over an extended period to meet them, then I am afraid you are not a good friend; you are either a bad friend or just a plain old acquaintance. Making time to meet someone is so important in deep, meaningful friendships. Not just that message on the phone every now and then, but a physical meeting especially if they are within an hour's travel from you.

I am not sure you can be a good friend of anyone who you could meet but choose not to make time to meet. Make and take time to meet people--they are more important for your happiness and well-being than your goals. What good is it having experiences in life if you have no one to share them with? On your death bed, the sub 4-minute mile you ran will not give you a hug or the model airplane you made won't make you laugh. So many people on their death beds list not spending time with their friends as their major life regret. Time with people you love is one key to happiness. Shared experiences are a true spice of life, they bring a smile to my face just to think of the fun times I have had with friends and it brings a warmth to my heart to think of how lucky I am to have the ability to choose to have more of these shared experiences in the future. Yes, spend your time on you, but also make time to spend with others, even though your savings account of time is consistently dwindling. Share it--it probably will make you happy.

Reach out to an old friend who was good for you. When is the right time to reach out to an old friend? Maybe they have moved on with life and will ignore your message. Another regret of the dying is truly wishing they cared less about what people think of them, in other words, if they don't return your call, maybe your unconscious decision to drift apart was the correct one. Good job, unconscious me. But it is a good idea to find out who you can truly count as friends. What is stopping you from doing it today? You are equipped with the knowledge that friendships should be cherished and you know that people who lose touch with friends regret doing so when they look back at their lives. Make a conscious decision; decide within a certain time frame you will reconnect with someone who was considered at one time a good friend. From this reaching out, you either regain contact with a friend or you confirm that drifting apart was correct move for both your lives. Enter the process with this attitude.

In order to make new friends or make acquaintance with a potential mate, you have got to make a decent first impression. One of the greatest challenges known to man is remembering someone's name when they tell you it at first meeting. Along with biting the inside of your mouth, this is just an amazing kink in evolution that shows us that humans still have a few failings. Maybe future generations will have wider cheeks and have greater listening skills. I think that I miss/forget the name I am being presented with because I am so intent on getting my own name right. Don't fuck that up because if you do, you will look like a right idiot during this first impression.

I am also focused on making sure I smile and shake hands with the perfect grip and vigor. Imagine having a confused facial expression while giving a lazy limp handshake. Who gives limp handshakes? How is that a thing? I am going to just open my hand, disengage the wrist and let you do all the shaking. It is like your arm after you have slept on it all night by mistake and is for the first minute of waking like a rubber chicken tied to your shoulder. Don't be a limp handshaker. If you take one thing from reading this book, it probably should be to become a more conscious decision maker in your life, but the second thing is to strengthen up any loose and limp handshakes.

Whether or not you like it, first impressions do matter quite a bit. People, unfortunately, are like the talent show panelist and have judged you on your general appearance before you speak, will then judge your handshake, your name, your voice, your teeth, your smile, your demeanor, your fragrance. As the conversation progresses, assuming your initial impressions has led to a follow-on conversation. People will judge your job, your friends, your car, your address, your accommodation, your hobbies, and your lifestyle. A lot of people, myself included, unconsciously get through a large majority of that list within the first few minutes of meeting someone. I find it almost impossible not to judge and form an early opinion even though I know I shouldn't. Judging is the lazy approach. It is far harder to be fully open minded and free from judgement. Some people think, once again the ego in us speaking, that we are excellent judges of character and that all our friends are amazing people and all those we find unbearable are terrible folk.

I have been described as a 'slow burner' to get to like which must be because of bad first impressions, more than likely because I'm initially obviously so intent on getting my name and handshake correct that I forget that the other person is telling me their name and possibly more information. Maybe I am just the asshole that some people think I am. Of course, I do not think this, I, on reflection, am shy.

Shyness in someone is seen as some form of weakness or in my case, arrogance, 'Look at him there, so arrogant, not speaking to us'. Shyness does not serve you when it comes to work or relationships—when usually the most charismatic, arrogant, and outgoing people in life are more likely to make an impression on others. They are remembered, and being remembered is important when trying to make connections. It is difficult to become 'unshy' or assertive. A conscious person who is aware of this can work on their assertiveness as a choice.

Assertiveness can get you through doors in life that shyness will keep locked. Shyness is a character trait that may be considered a character flaw. A flaw that is hard to be rid of, but with a conscious mind and practice of being assertive then assertiveness can become the norm. An assertive person is calm, a good listener, reasonable, polite and a good communicator. All these are not traits of an asshole unless you take assertiveness to mean being obnoxious. An obnoxious person is loud, aggressive, refuses to listen, egotistical, and stubborn. We can choose between obnoxious, shy, or assertive.

Develop your story every day when someone asks you "how was your day?" or "what did you get up to at the weekend?". Say something--most people enjoy hearing anything other than the lazy answers, 'good', 'fine', 'ah not much, yourself'. Be consistently evocative in the art of the short conversation. These short connections are important, the lazy amongst us will dismiss these. This engagement makes you an interesting person. A person someone gets recommended to others to meet, because you are something unlike the 'fine' person who can seem to have no substance.

Remember, you are a living, breathing human who is engaging in the world and the people around you. Personally, I find this difficult. Engaging with strangers is not something that comes easily to me. I am aware of it and have been trying to improve in this area by being more outgoing. A sort of fake it 'til you make it approach. If this is your struggle, too, it is worth it to try and come out of your shell. Connections are opportunities to learn, love and grow. Maybe today is the day to start to make a new effort in your connections.

8 DETERMINATION

Write a book presuming no one will read it. Take a photo not to impress people on social media. Exercise, not because you want to look good for others, but to feel good about yourself. Do things and don't tell anyone--do it for you and only you. Draw a picture and don't share it. Write a journal entry and don't tell anyone. Do things in the silent bask of self-satisfaction and achievement. Your goals are for you, not for anyone else. If you achieve your goals, only share if asked--your goals must be for you.

If you need external motivation for doing, think of your children (if you have any) or future children (if you want any), they will be conditioned by your activities. Your children watch your every move and learn by your actions. If you are a couch dweller and a screen addict your children will have more of a disposition towards those things. If you are lazy, well then your kids will be......? If you are a person who thinks they can inspire their children through words, you are probably sadly mistaken. You have a responsibility to young people who spend time in your presence to be a better you. if you want your children to read, you need to read, if you want your children to have fun, you must have fun, if you want your children to exercise, you have got to go exercise.

Jim Carrey had it right in that film, Yes Man, where he would say "yes" all the time. If you were to do it, that would make for quite the interesting life, wouldn't it? I'd imagine things would get weird, fast. You would say 'yes' all day and it would lead you into a spiral of bad decisions and end up with you giving your life savings to a hooker to feed her heroin habit in exchange for.... well let's just say you probably wouldn't be getting value for money.

Saying yes more in life leads to more opportunities. It is a weapon in your armory. Use it wisely. Most people don't say it enough and miss out on the experiences, adventures, and stories because they want to remain in the safety of the lazy zone. That lazy zone is a scary place to find yourself constantly in--scary, because if you think of it, spending day after day without leaving that zone means you are not experiencing all the joys life has to offer. Without experiencing the joys of life, are you really living life or just been a passive passenger taking for granted your time here on Earth? This is what is scary--a wasted life.

Of course, this is just my perspective. Every man and woman the world considers great, was a doer. They said yes to challenges and opportunities and made something of themselves. If you consciously decide to remain in that lazy zone, you have committed to being an uninteresting passenger in life.

When on your death bed someone asks you to tell your life story so they can write your book to read to your grandchildren, how would it read? "My grandmother was awesome," your grandson could say, or "my grandmother didn't really do much." Even in this made-up scenario, think how proud you would be telling your story. Or would you be slightly embarrassed by your lack of adventures? You might be thinking at that point with your life ending about your regrets. Regrets stem generally from the things you didn't do rather than the things you have done.

Now is the time to decide to consciously say yes to more experiences and people. You never know where it might take you, but one thing to remember: it should make your life story a more awesome read and make you the most interesting character in it. It really does depend on what the offer is, though. Is it yes to another beer? Yes, to a week of silent meditation? Of those two, which would be better for you and an experience that could change your life? Sometimes, of course, the offer is never there, and the question is never asked; you must go find the thing to say yes to. So, yes, go be Jim Carey in Yes Man for a while, just avoid the hookers and the drugs, OK? If you are going to say yes more you still must be able and willing to say NO, and that can be more difficult.

Fucking willpower, the lost art of determination and discipline. The opposite to saying yes is no, duh! Captain Obvious strikes again. You must believe in the choices and goals that you have set for yourself and not be taken away from these targets by a need to say yes to societal or other pressures. In many situations in my life, I have succumbed to the pressure of yes. Sometimes saying yes is the lazy approach. Doing things that I knew were wrong for me. I was unconsciously falling into the peer pressure trap. The times I didn't study so I would play computer games or skip exercise to have beers. These are low level choices, but they have high repercussions when repeated.

You decide to follow a path of pressure when you have already set aside that time to say yes to yourself. You can't double yes; you have inadvertently said yes to one and no to the other. You have reprioritized your life, putting computers and beer before your goals. Now if making new friends or getting a new high score is your goal, off you go. But if it isn't, you achieve first and say yes but only after you are satisfied with your productivity plan. Maybe saying yes to your goal and ambition requires the ability to say a full NO to the activity that isn't part of where you are going. But there must be a balance; your goals are not everything. Don't lose sight of your relationships. What is the true cost of achieving your goal?

There is, of course, the argument that you would or could lose out on friends with the NO approach. What is a friend really if they don't respect and know you enough to say that you got your shit together and you will go for the beer once you get your priorities covered? Surround yourself with people who can do both. Get their priorities covered and shoot the shit. In an ideal world, you can probably do both things if you have the time. That is where your time management skills come into play. You set aside two hours on arrival home from work to finish your research project and go for a quick run before you socialize. You oversee your schedule and time, plan it. Fitting your goals into that schedule along with your relaxing time is a balance you can look for.

Get your shit together, conscious human. Does your life need a metaphorical shake? Seriously, where do you see yourself in a few years? Maybe you're not entirely sure? Ok, where do you see yourself in a year? Kind of know, but not really, probably realistically doing the same things you are doing now. Are you a normal person who does normal things? In your head that's fine, you have made peace with the fact that you are doing OK, you go to the gym every now and then, you read when you feel like it and you pay the bills. You are cruising through life. But are you going nowhere? What are your steps to be the best you? Have you interest in seeing what the best you looks like? A genuine question. Some people find happiness in hours of TV and cruising through a lazy unchallenging life. Maybe that's a goal? The ability to do nothing with nothing could be a goal. During your empty time are you happy with just you and your mind? Can you enjoy this space without the need for materialism? This could be the hardest goal of all. Maybe that would be the best you.

Goals, of course, are not the answer to all life's problems. Without a doubt, they can sometimes be used to extremes and people miss out on daily pleasure in search of this huge goal in their life. This could ruin a vast majority of their life, as they have put aside many daily pleasures to get to this end goal. Will the end goal lead to the ultimate joy and happiness? It probably won't. Achieving a major goal does give oneself an inner pride and satisfaction but if it comes at a cost of relationships, family, friends, joys and experiences over a sustained period, is it worth it?

Goals must be sustainable within a life that gives you joy. Doing something so the future you can look back maybe on your death bed with pride is great but maybe the future you will look back and say that was wasted time that you should have spent with your friends which you ended up losing, chasing the goal. With the goals you set, remember they should come with changes to your current regimes but not at the cost of all your current happiness.

The process of the goal should be an enjoyable one. Enjoy exercise, enjoy drawing, enjoy reading, enjoy research, enjoy what you are studying, and enjoy the experience but not at a significant cost to your happiness.

A woman told me last year why she gave up running. She had a set of exams coming up, important exams she needed to do well in. She, as a result, gave up her habit of running 4 times a week to concentrate on the exams. I asked her how long she usually spent from start to finish during these running sessions. About 90 minutes was the answer. So, I asked her why she chose to give up on this activity which has been proved to help with brain function instead of the social media time, Netflix time, YouTube time that she continues with? She was aware she had made this choice, but she made it unconsciously.

What was this choice about? Everyone has made a similar choice in their life. She gave up the wrong thing to pursue her goals, she also cost herself a lot of happiness, so was the goal worthwhile at this cost? Only she can answer that but at the time she was a very unhappy version of herself and admitted to being hugely stressed. She was so stressed in fact she had begun to see a psychologist about it. Would she have been happier with including her running goal alongside her success in exams goal? Maybe she would have been happier without any exam?

This happens a lot in modern education where sometimes the end goal has totally replaced the process. In many minds, the process of learning is only a vehicle to get them through an exam, cram the information into a short-term memory pile just long enough to get through this 3-hour paper. The end goal of the final exam often comes at the cost of a child's mental health. The pressure we as the world and more specifically, overanxious parents, put on teenagers is ruining the true potential of the education system. Parents sometimes see the success of their child as making up for their own failings.

Maybe the parent remembers him- or herself being lazy at school and skipping study sessions to chill out with friends--they did it then because it made them happy, but happiness of their own child can take a back seat. The true cost of this pressure is of course difficult to measure. You can take yourself to the Scandinavian working model, where statistically they have the shortest workday but have great productivity. The same in education it is not the number of hours, it is the quality of the process of learning during those hours. A child's mind needs to relax, play and make social connections so all these should be part of a child's 'goals' as well as the exam results. Unless the path to the end goal of amazing school test scores is an enjoyable and rewarding experience, it will come at the cost up maybe 4 or 5 years of gloom. A childhood of gloom chasing these goals will not lead to an adulthood of success and happiness. Be conscious of the cost to daily happiness in any goal you set, especially if you are setting them for others in your care.

Let's presume you are walking on the road of good intentions--there is a reason it has affinity with the road to hell. If you have intent to achieve a goal without strategy, it is a pile of turd. You aren't going to do it. It is very similar to going to the gym without a plan: you go to the gym you enter the gym and then what happens is a 'let me see' kind of wander around with no link to previous or future sessions. This gym attempt is, yes, better than no gym visit, but you can be infinitely more productive with your time if you are following a plan. This may sound obvious, but many people attack their goals without a plan. Fail to prepare, prepare to fail.

"I am going to write a book" was my personal favorite. I kept saying to myself, 'yes, I will write a book' 'it will be so good' 'I have a great idea for a book'. Saying it made me feel good about myself, I was going to do it, you know, but just not now. I am busy now. But when I made a strategy and small achievable goals that didn't negatively affect my daily happiness, it started working, I started writing and continued. This led to increased happiness because I enjoyed the process. Turns out, I liked writing. My hobby that I tried to do turned into a passion. Many hobbies I have tried, haven't. Look to scuba diving, videography, powerlifting and drawing. I am perfectly fine with each failed hobby not taking me to Passionville, USA. Passion is a thrown-about word. It really is just the hobbies you are determined to spend the most time doing. I became passionate about writing. How did I manage this?

Well, because I enjoyed achieving little goals--the 500 words and 1000-word goals. I got a sense of satisfaction. The sense of joy was even greater because it came at no cost to my general lifestyle. I placed my writing into set time slots in my life that I was alone for anyway but maybe would have been unproductive. So now my productivity brought me happiness. Of course, I often didn't feel like writing and that is where the rewards come in. I said to myself just do the 500 words and then you can watch all the lazy TV you want. If I left it to when I felt like it my laziness gene would kick in and it would never get done. The words would be achieved during my set period hence the goal is achieved, and I got to do the chill out thing with no guilt, just satisfaction.

Merge your goals into your daily practices at set times, make them short at first so you don't feel burdened by the process. Eventually, you may start to enjoy and process and spend more time doing it. The challenge now is to set this month's goals, write them down, and put them above or beside your screen (tv, laptop, phone). Screen time is the time your mind can wander, let it wander to your goals and then turn off Instagram and remind yourself to achieve first. The phone might be your worst habit, but habits are not all bad-- in fact, they are the key to achieving goals and enjoying the process.

'The Power of Habit' by Charles Duhigg is a book I recommend reading. It suggests that bad habits can linger because they are not replaced. For example, a simple habit like biting your nails is hard to eliminate because your mind automatically goes to it, whereas you can consciously choose to change the habit, and every time you go to bite your nails, to replace it with chewing gum. Bad habits need to be replaced and good habits need to be implemented into your routine. Maybe you need to replace some of your lazy habits like me?

Habits come into effect every day and every moment of your life. We are trained to work on autopilot almost. Moving from task to task using muscle memory and only tuning in and out sporadically to check it is all going OK. Think of the drive to work-- how much of it do you remember doing every day? When you first learned to drive, it was a massive stressful brain-taxing exercise. It now is mundane, automatic, a habit, and forgotten.

An issue with habits is that it is so easy to form and maintain bad habits. Simple things like if we are trying to lose weight but every time we have a cup of coffee we have a habit of eating a few cookies with it, they go hand in hand in our mind. But there is no actual link between the two, other than a habit that formed years ago, and we have nothing to replace the cookie with.

Bad habits are not just restricted to, or as obvious as, a

poor diet. I see bad habits as a reflection of how we spend our time. Your day can probably be separated into good and bad habits. Reflect on today or yesterday. How much time was spent on what you can refer to as good habits when you have the choice? You decide what is a good habit for you. Can you replace some of the bad habits with good habits that serve you? For instance, while writing this piece I picked up my phone twice to check Instagram. Why did I do this? It was a subconscious act. I didn't even remember twice deciding to do it. I just became fully aware when I was already on the phone. I now have formed a habit loop of when I am writing, and have a little thinking time, I switch to the bloody phone to fill my head space. This is a bad habit for me. The empty time where the next idea could come from has been filled by the screen. This I have recognized as a bad habit. I will replace the phone by my side with a notebook and leave my phone out of reach when I am typing. Simple solution. The only reason I thought of this is that I am trying to be a conscious human and make conscious choices when it comes to my time. No longer will I be a slave to the lazy screens. I will replace them in many aspects of my life.

Have a habit audit immediately. Think about how your day is structured and what are the automatic things you do every day. From how you turn off your alarm in the morning to when you switch off your light at night. Take your time, either by writing down or by just thinking about your daily routine. Now think about what things you would like to do as part of your routine and what things in your routine do not serve you. Think about setting in place your morning habit loop from alarm to leaving the house. I know I have my routine which I do change up slightly every now and then. At the moment I wake at 5am (I will get to this early wake up time later), straight to making coffee, smoothie and oats while listening to an audio book, I switch on my hot water, I then take my coffee, smoothie, and laptop and begin writing. I used to have my phone with me but now, as mentioned earlier, I will leave it in the other room as it really distracts from me from being productive. I write for an hour, then I have a shower put on my work clothes and out the door for 6.50am. Once at work, I check my emails while having my second coffee of the day and I set out my to do list on my weekly page and that's when I begin make decisions that are out of my routine, only at around 7.30am do I do the first thing out of routine (habit) that is two and a half hours after getting up. Two and half hours of automatic.

This is automatic but all the decisions I made to fill this routine have been made consciously. I avoid having to make on the spot decisions as for me, in the morning, a lazy and maybe unhealthy choice could be made for convenience. Every decision does not need to be conscious in every part of your day, as that would be exhausting. Weighing up decisions consciously and then implementing that decision many times as part of a routine means that routine becomes paradoxically conscious yet unconscious.

The things I am proud of in my automatic mornings are; I have eaten healthy food, I have produced some writing, I have listened to a book and I have set my goals for the day. If I had to decide every morning what to do, would I have been as productive as I have been? Probably not. Nail your routine down, especially the morning one, think about what type of human you are and what your goals and ambitions are and then set in place a system where you cannot fail. Make it easy to succeed, make it easy for you to be a better conscious human. Don't drift through life letting mundane decisions tax your brain. Make the mundane decisions now and make them so you are achieving something with your time whether it is exercise, reading, writing, drawing, singing, meditation, or yoga. Do what makes you happy. What is the first step to all this? Get up early sunshine, get up early.

Early starts are the key to an amazing morning. This is the time that can separate you from the masses. You can choose to get up earlier and have an extra two hours for you. You might say that means you must go to bed super early. You are correct--to facilitate my 5am starts, I am in bed before 10pm most nights. But there is a massive difference between having two hours in the morning to yourself versus two hours at 9 o' clock at night. At night you are automatically lazy and for me I would waste these late hours on screens. The two hours in the morning are the best two hours of the day. Give it to yourself, not to your boss. Invest the first two hours of work in yourself, treat it like your other job. This job is all about yourself. You are far more productive at that time than you would be after a day's work, that is why I tend to save the exercise I do until after work. I exercise when my mind is tired, but my body still needs to be challenged.

With the early start, I would recommend doing the unconscious, previously-decided tasks first, the ones that you do automatically, like making your food or ironing, whatever needs to be done. I do these while listening to an audio book as mentioned already. It takes me about 20 minutes to complete these tasks, then I am awake enough to do whatever it is I have set as part of my routine. Now, it is writing, but this can change. I set myself up in a comfortable and inspiring environment, I make it a pleasure. Somedays I am not very productive during this time I have set aside. But it is the routine of it, even if I only write 100 words, I have maintained the habit and thus the cycle of productivity has continued.

I use an A4 page taped to my desk to help my in-work laziness. This is the productivity tool I learned from an off-hand comment from a school principal I met. He said that he would have a page on his desk and split the page into 4 categories, important and urgent, not important but urgent, not urgent but important, and not important not urgent. Every to-do item that he was faced with could fit into one of those categories. A useful tool to prioritize your productivity. I have taken it a step forward, every Friday when I finished work, the last thing I do is tidy and clean my desk for the week ahead. Then I will take out one of my preprinted pages of productivity and stick it with tape to my desk and begin filling in the sections for the next week. Each day has several set tasks that I need to complete and then has a section for a to-do list. Each day I set out what the plan is. I take less and less time to think about what I must do. I just do what is on the list. Of course, this is just a glorified to-do list, but to-do lists work. You can make yours even better than mine-- lay it out in a way that works for you.

On the sheet I have the 4 (important/urgent) areas laid out for larger and more long-term tasks that I fill in each Friday. There is a general notes area and a calendar of the month. The outside becomes a place to take phone numbers, emails, or even the odd doodle. This page has increased my productivity--no longer do I search for a to-do list, it is always there, every time I have finished a task. I cross it off and continue to a new one. The crossing off tasks alone makes me feel a small bit of pride and purpose which will focus me onto the next task. This can be done on your computer or a phone but there is something about the physicality of the sheet and the constant awareness of it always being in view. It is there to keep me being productive so I can finish tasks on time and allow me to have as much time as possible away from the office and as little time thinking about the office when I am at home.

I work hard during my time at work, but I will not let it consume me. I am under no illusion that if I dropped dead in the morning I would be replaced within the week. Some other minion will fill my shoes. My ego is itching to say, as I write this, that my replacement couldn't be as good as me, but realistically, they could, and maybe would, be better than me. Are you, like me, replaceable in what you do? One of the biggest death bed regrets is 'I wish I hadn't worked so hard'. Is it worth it? The stress, the deadlines, the emails, for what? Your ego to be massaged with 'Employee of the Month' and other minor life incentives. 'You know it's just nice be recognized'. Here is an idea, commit to yourself first instead of committing to a person/company who has bought your time. See that long-term project through.

I think it was Darren Hardy who said, 'Commitment is doing the thing you said you were going to do long after the mood you said it in has left you'. We are the generation of the quick fix, the 7-day weight loss, the learn Spanish in a day, 5 simple steps, we love thinking we can master something in a matter in days. Do these 10 exercises for chiseled abs. What happened to good things comes to those who wait? So many of my ideas have fallen through the cracks of commitment when the moment has passed where I thought it was an awesome idea. The effort of it all when it comes to going through the steps. For instance, I have always thought I wanted to learn Arabic, but it's difficult so I have given up despite starting multiple times. The initial commitment to the idea only served me as far as the first couple of tries, then it was slowly replaced with 'this is too hard' and excuses. Let's go back to the comfort of doing fuck all. Ahhhhh. Why would I even bother testing my mind? When do I even need it? I have got on fine this far without having it. I have fully justified being too lazy to learn the language to myself and therefore it will now disappear from my consciousness until I come up with the great idea again.

How many of my good ideas have been thrown on the rubbish pile due to lack of commitment following an initial surge? My life is littered with them. Remember that café I was going to open, the farm land in Brazil I was going to buy, the wedding band I was going to start, the fitness app I was going to design, the YouTube channel that was ready to go and the math gaming site I was going to design? All these ideas lie in the scrap heap in the back of my mind. Lost to time, lost to laziness, due to lack of strategy and commitment. Maybe some were shit ideas and I didn't have the skill or ability to back them up. Did I even really try though? Did I put more than 3 hours into any of them? Did I go beyond the first step? When I look back now, I can see that I these ideas are gone maybe for the better but maybe they would have been the different path in my life and changed it totally. But I feel that for many of my ideas, I didn't give them the time and effort that they deserved, I just threw them away because they were out of my comfort zone at the time or the mood was gone.

9 PREVENTION

Why isn't everyone fit and healthy? Why don't people sleep well? With fitness and health, is the problem a lack of education in the skill of staying fit and healthy? Is it a problem that starts at home as a child and is continued in school and polished off in adulthood? The Education in schools revolves around the abstain model and the food pyramid diagram. A bit like the classic "drugs are bad" from SouthPark. Sugar is bad, fast food is bad, and trans fats are bad, mm-kay. Saying a thing is bad to teenagers is the greatest student engagement switch off you will ever see in a classroom. Educate the youth on the "good" way, the path to enlightenment. The deliciousness of good food and the feeling you get from eating it. The importance of preparation and routine in eating and not just the importance of the food itself.

Unfortunately, when we tune into the world of nutrition online, we are subjected to the adverts of those who wish to make money off us. The quick fix shake, tea, smoothie, powder, pill or suppository. Ah, yes, exactly what I need, fit tea, that'll solve everything. That expert from Celebrity Love Island or the Bachelorette, who obviously is my 'body goal', is promoting it and they look amazing. Don't, as a conscious human, be fooled by the shit that is thrown at you to lose weight or get healthy. Instead, think unprocessed food, fresh fruit and vegetables, nuts seeds and meat or fish. Load up on the good stuff, the vegetables. You will feel like a fucking champion. It is your body, think of the fuel you are putting in. You know what it should be, you know it deep inside, so do it. Unfortunately, laziness trumps health for many people, that fast food is just too easy.

Eating like a child is a problem for adults. We use food as the reward for success and failure. Oh, I had a tough day at work, let's get a big-assed pizza and ice cream. I got the promotion let's eat cake. Nothing overly wrong with the goods in question but it is a problem when it becomes a crutch that turns to a daily habit of eating like the 10-year-old. 'I want to eat cake, I am big now, so I will eat it, all the time'. There is no one there to tell you "not until you finish your vegetables" or "just one slice". When you listen to your inner 10-year-old, you are still a child. Grow up. If you feel unhealthy or are overweight, you are one of four things:

1. Someone who knows a bit about nutrition and chooses to ignore
2. Someone who knows nothing about nutrition and chooses not to learn
3. Someone who knows a lot about nutrition but is too lazy to implement
4. Someone who knows a lot about nutrition but chooses to stay unhealthy.

But if you know it is unhealthy, you know it is slowly killing you. Why do people do this? Because you are eating like a child. You are an adult, eat like one for fuck's sake.

Can you imagine the Simpsons and good old Homer wolfing down the latest chow served up by the uber-loyal Marge? This process is the exact opposite of Mindful Eating -- the enjoyment and savoring of the food. If you are in the habit of the Homer Simpson model of eating, you are possibly missing out on the true taste and flavor of the food. You are seeing food only as a fuel to be consumed, maybe later, when full, you sit back and 'enjoy' some chocolate or ice cream. Hunger takes away from the enjoyment of food for some as they cannot stop themselves from 'Homer Simpsoning' it down. A conscious eater is one who enjoys the experience of eating and is present throughout the eating. Think of subconsciously eating popcorn in the cinema, an automatic stuffing of your face. Are you enjoying each bite or are you just' metronoming' the experience as you take in the film? When you eat your meals are you in front of a television 'metronoming' the food? Do you fully chew and taste each bit if you are at the dinner table? Is your food gone in 3 minutes flat? Slow down, take conscious control of your eating experience, you have control. Put your cutlery down a few times during eating. Drink water between bites. Enjoy each bite, slowly.

That control can also be lost as the reins get away from you with the amount you eat. You will always finish the plate. For some it is from childhood, I think, where parents wouldn't allow them to leave the table without finishing every bite. As I am conscious of my decisions, I can change this, surely, but it's easier said than done, isn't it? The food comes out in a restaurant and, hey presto, the plate is clean. I almost suffered through the last quarter of the dish to make sure I finished it. I couldn't possibly waste the food.

There are some strategies to overcome this, for example, at home, use smaller plates and at restaurants, ask the server to put half the portion in a takeaway box before it gets to the table. It's amazing we must go to these lengths to eat less, but we do. Most of us when given food will on 'automatic brain mode' overeat. This is most likely a nod to our ancestors who, for example, when coming across a tree with abundant apples, would first stuff themselves and then collect as much as they could for eating later, of course not knowing when they would eat again. For some of us this is still our automatic. We should be in total control of our eating, our minds can overwrite this automatic program. For your next meal, stop when you are full, or when you think you are full, even with the intention of resuming in a few minutes. Wait a few minutes and see if you want to continue, be conscious as to if you have eaten enough. If you are full then stop. Some call this willpower and maybe it is, just a case of semantics, but it really is your conscious mind telling your unconscious that you don't need to overeat because you know there is another meal in a few hours.

"Diet" is a word that is scary and comes with a lot of negative feelings of restriction and suffering. Diets, when associated with quick fixes, fail, however lifestyle changes and sustainable habits work. "Diet" suggests, and usually means, to restrict yourself and deny yourself. You change everything usually all at once. You don't want to do this forever, you just want to lose a few pounds. Just lose a few pounds, then what? Back to the old ways, of course, and the weight comes back. Once again, we knew this before we started, didn't we? But we still did it, because we convinced ourselves that this time it will be different. I am going to do it. But once again, it goes so well for about a week and then it gets hard and we slip a few times and then we just go back to the old ways. That diet doesn't work. Or we do well, and we do lose the weight. Congratulations, we look amazing for that wedding or party or holiday. But then once the photos are taken with our sucked-in gut and newly-starved physique we go back at it, cake and pizza and don't hold the sprinkles and parmesan.

Grazing unconsciously is a major problem when it comes to staying in shape, or more importantly, staying healthy. By adding this extra fat to your body, you are highly increasing your chances of clogging arteries, heart disease, diabetes, strokes, cancer and high blood pressure (by no means an exhaustive list). So why do you eat the shit food? Because it tastes good, because it is there, and because it is what I always do. We can't be satisfied with this relationship with food. We shouldn't be satisfied with this relationship with food. So, change it. You oversee what goes in your food hole. Seriously, think now about your relationship with food. What are your bad habits? What are your good habits? Chuck a shitload of vegetables in every meal and replace the bad habits with loads of healthy shit. Prepare, prepare, prepare. That's the key--buy the fruits and veg so they are there in the fridge, make your own dinners and lunches, know what goes in your food. You can still eat the pizza or whatever you enjoy as long it is part of a majority healthy eating routine. Enjoy the feeling of healthy fresh food as you fuel. Your energy will increase, and your body and mind will thank you. Your relationship with food must be conscious of the consequences of your food choices. You will feel like shit if you eat like an unconscious lazy spoilt child.

The cost myth of eating right is just that it is a myth. Go down to the store and you will see they are practically giving the good stuff away. That fresh section of the store is full of deals and goodness. The price of eating out and ordering in is more than the monetary cost. Think about the physical cost to your body--that's the real cost. Even if you think it is cheaper to eat the unhealthy way, are you saying you don't realize that burger and fries you are shoveling down your gob is bad for you? Today, the fact that fast and processed food is bad for you is as obvious as the negative effect of smoking and alcohol. Yet the world is getting fatter, the knowledge is being ignored. Maybe we need the public shame offensive that hit smoking with the taxes and the bans. Maybe we need the state to intervene because we are too weak minded to resist. People who smoke are made to pay huge taxes for their unhealthy ways in many countries, as it is a serious problem for public health. Maybe this is because it can negatively affect others by inhaling someone else's smoke. However, the obesity problem is crippling nations' health systems. Now might be the time to increase the tax on unhealthy foods and decrease the tax on the healthy ones. For example, see the soda tax in the US. Maybe we need the nanny state to say no for us because we are too used to saying yes to our inner spoilt lazy child.

Healthy eating, as with exercise which I will get to later, must be implemented through a set of daily habits. This is to ensure your healthy eating is a routine, not a chore. You always eat healthily because it is easier than eating rubbish and tastes better. I have a morning routine that involves eating a smoothie while I make coffee and porridge for my second breakfast later. I load the smoothie with goodness (fruits and vegetables) and make my oats delicious with fruits and cinnamon. Easy, simple, unconscious routine that is so much harder to break now than complete. I have made it easier to eat right in the morning than to eat wrong. Make it easier by maybe shopping online and having much fruit and vegetables delivered to your door. If you don't have time to make you own food, and can afford it, set up a meal subscription service than will tailor-make healthy meals and deliver them to you.

Plan your meals in advance, make salads in bulk for your next day's lunch as well as today's dinner. Make them packed with nutrition and delicious so you enjoy it too. When you make your own meals, you have the benefit of seeing exactly what is in it. When you go to a restaurant, foods can taste amazing because you don't see the 3 magic restaurant ingredients they put in everything-- butter, salt and sugar. Restaurants only want you to have a taste sensation, so you keep coming back for more, they don't give two shits about the calorie content or health benefits. Also, in restaurants they have a standard size no matter what your size, if you are a 300lb lumberjack or a 150lb office worker you will be given the same pasta dish. Must you eat it all?

Leave behind your snacking ways and join the celery brigade. No way, man, I love my cookies and chips. Nutrition is like fuel for your car; you can't put diesel in a petrol car and expect top performance. High-sugar food, however, is like putting rocket fuel into a Fiat 500, except a lot of times, the Fiat 500 is sat on the couch watching Game of Thrones. This high-calorie, high-energy food is hence stored as fat for when winter is coming. Of course, when winter does come, instead of fighting off the White Walkers, we sit on the couch again and stuff our faces while watching Suits. She is a princess now, you know.

Your mind will justify the instantaneous pleasure, it will forget the previous goals you had set for yourself, and will throw out the window the future plans of glorious health and wellbeing for this one moment of eating an ice cream sundae after a pizza while watching America's Got Talent reruns. For some reason, our mind is set to sabotage when it comes to this type of choice. Our mind rejects logic and replaces it with lazy justification for what you are about to eat. It must be a hard wiring from our ancestors when comfort and calories were an unattainable luxury which we strived towards. High calories meant survival back in knuckle-dragging times, now high calories means chronic disease. The 'it's OK to gorge myself' button in our minds is always on the verge of being switched on. You deserve it you had a tough day. Bullshit, a tough day means you should refuel properly, otherwise you'll just feel shittier.

Have healthy snacks as the easy-to-find option, have apples and oranges ready to eat when you need a sugar hit. It is when you do not have a routine of eating that you make and allow yourself to make the decision to eat unhealthily, because it is easier, and it is what is advertised. Wake up to the fact that you control what goes into your mouth, you have a choice of a small, instant pleasure or a longer satisfaction pleasure. Remember you are a choice- making conscious human; make decisions that your future self will appreciate, and you will live a longer healthier life for it. You will feel better. Take charge of your life and what fuel you put in your body, take charge now. Set your routines, put some time now into planning what you will eat for the week, make it so it is harder to fail.

Calculate your BMR (Basal Metabolic Rate) and track your eating. Do you know how many calories you should eat a day? This is different to BMI (Body Mass Index) which only is a simplistic ratio of height and weight to deem if you are overweight or not. BMI is not overly reliable, but can be used as an indicator to see if you are technically overweight. Back to BMR. You can calculate that, right? Well luckily for you, you can just type it into Google and it will direct you to a BMR calculation website. It is not a flawless system, but it is a guide you can use along with a calorie tracker to see how much you need to eat in order to stay or get in shape. You will need to input your gender, age, activity level, height, and weight and it will churn out the number of calories that would be your maintenance calories for a day. Maintenance calories is an estimation of the number of calories you can consume in order to keep weight the same, so no weight loss or gain with this number of calories. If you haven't done this before, put down the book and do it now. You should be hugely interested in this number.

What to do with this number? Now you should for a while do the dreaded but extremely useful calorie tracking. This can be done once again with the help of technology (what a world we live in), you can use an app such as MyFitnessPal to track your calories daily. A lot of us will say we don't have the energy, interest, or time to do this every day, but you only need to do it for a few typical days to see what your typical daily caloric intake comes to. The amazing thing about this is you can pinpoint exactly (if this is a problem) where you are over-consuming calories.

You must put everything you eat and drink into the app, though, you need to be very aware about all snacking, everything that you consume counts. If you find you are eating more calories than your BMR rate, you will gain weight, if you are eating less than your BMR, you will lose weight. You can throw all other fads, weight loss pills and diet supplement out the window, the mathematics is simple and correct. A caloric deficit is the only thing that will lead to weight loss.

You will be a fit and healthy person in ten years because of the decisions you made today, or you will be living between doctors' appointments and medication for high blood pressure, wondering how it came to this. Wake up and be conscious, you can prevent this, prevent your future suffering by fixing your day-to-day intake now. Make the fruits and vegetables easy to eat and the chocolate a chore. Write down your intention each week to eat an exact amount of fruit and veg before you can touch any chocolate. Once again, it goes back to habit and routine; you can stop it if you are conscious. Focus on what you want to eat while you watch TV or play Fortnite, have that ingrained and associated with the activity, replace the former bad eating habit with a new I will snack on this instead. Don't become a member of the unconscious snacking society, be free to choose what you consume in the knowledge it will make you healthier and probably happier.

Hydration is the key, didn't you know? Yawn. We all know to drink more water and cut out the sodas and alcohol. But sodas are delicious, and alcohol is so much fun, you say. Socially drinking can be enjoyable and relaxing, but like anything, moderation is the key. You are a conscious living thing that cannot be forced to consume anything, but you, like me, enjoy the consumption of alcohol. Create strategies for limiting the negative effect of alcohol on your health by introducing water as a drink to consume alongside alcohol, setting limits and sticking to them or drinking healthier drinks. Hydration post and pre-alcohol is a good idea and have your post alcohol food premade as something healthy not the dive into the nearest McDonalds. As fully-grown adults, we can make the decision to consume alcohol, but it is that, a decision. The amount we consume should be consciously controlled and thought about. Just, with anything that enters your body, you are in control.

You are also in control of what you do with your body and all that energy you have received from food. It's time to exercise, let's gooooo, and that's the next chapter.

10 EXERCISE

The most obvious thing in the world is to exercise. Sometimes, the hardest thing in the world is to exercise. Everyone knows the benefits of exercise but so many people ignore it, pass it off, and postpone it. It is difficult and goes against some ingrained ancient human trait of saving energy. The key to the prevention of many illness is to be fit. We have the recipe for wellbeing. Find me a successful and happy person who doesn't exercise in some way. It is remarkable how it is ignored by so many people.

You are aware of the need to exercise, but you don't exercise. Why the fuck not? The general reason must be because you do not enjoy the process. You hate the burpees, the weights, the running, the cycling and the stretching. Ugh, the thoughts of it. The effort. It is seen as a torture by many. How can you continue to do something that you do not see the instant rewards for? It is like taking a shower and not feeling clean after it. Would you still take a shower or look for something else that instantly works to clean yourself? The same happens with exercise, it takes a long time for your body to adapt to regular exercise. Your beach body won't be seen instantly. If you look in the mirror pre- and post-exercise your body probably will even look worse after exercise, all sweaty with a big red face. The results aren't instantaneous so we cannot enjoy them initially. We need to enjoy the process, but how? We need to love moving our body, testing our body and using our body in different ways.

The reward is not the beach body--some see this as the exercise goal. I want to have a six pack. I want to have more 'tone' in my arms. These are not the right reasons to exercise. It is like me saying I want to have a book written by me, but I don't want to be a writer. I want the product goal, but I do not want the process. Exercise must be broken down into mini goals, weekly and daily objectives. Track your progress, see how your speed, endurance and strength has improved each day. Make it quantifiable so if you cannot see the results instantly in your body you still can see the results in other ways. Place the goals somewhere you can always see them. And reward yourself when you see them through.

Set yourself challenges, test your body and see what it can do. No matter what your age weight and abilities, you can test your body. Can you do 10 burpees, if you can ok can you do 100? How long do they take you? Can you beat that at another time next month? OK, easy now, can you do 1000? Completed it, mate. Yup, that is an actual conversation I had in my head during an empty time thinking session. I made myself do 1000 burpees just because. What's your challenge to yourself going to be? Become a master of your body. It is amazing what it can do. Test it.

You hear stories of people achieving amazing things,

feats of endurance, fitness, or strength. One example I can think of--and someone you may not have heard of--is Ross Edgley. If you don't know who he is, he set out in his mind at one stage to swim around Great Britain. He went to extreme lengths to see if his body could do it. He succeeded, although his tongue did start falling apart from the seawater, but he succeeded. He wasn't a particularly talented swimmer, but he had a mindset of pushing his limits. Have you ever pushed yours?

You will never be younger than you are today so why not see can you run that 5km, 10km, Marathon. Ross Edgley is now onto his next challenge, with a fully recovered tongue. His swim is of course an extreme challenge, but everything you haven't achieved before is a challenge. Whether it is running a mile or swimming a length, completing the challenge is a success. Take satisfaction in each of your successes. Share them if you must, inspire others to do the same. Be the type of person who gets out of their comfort zone and tries new exercises and pushes the limits of you. Consciously decide now to achieve something this week, some feat you have never done before that is possible for you to do, you just haven't done it yet.

During my time writing this piece, I decided to try a few of these challenges. I set myself a month to achieve 6 fitness goals that I had never done before. I wanted to make exercise no longer a mundane process but an exciting challenge. The possibility of failure made it more interesting. The challenges I picked were, in this order: 1000 pushups, row half a marathon, run a half marathon, 1000 air squats, 1000 burpees (as mentioned above), climb 100 flights of stairs, and lunge walk 1 kilometer. How was my experience? Mentally very tough, for each I had to do a few practices in training during the first two weeks of the month. I tested my techniques and standards for each movement. Once I felt I had the movement down, I set a date and attempted.

The toughest mentally was the burpees, I felt utterly exhausted throughout the process, I had never completed more than 200 in any one workout so 5 times that amount was a physical challenge. The mental challenge was the constant chirp in my ear of the give-up devil. He was saying just rest, it's not worth it, who cares. But who was I doing it for? I was doing it for me, to test myself, so I continued and finished in a slow but successful time of 3 hours 11 minutes 55 seconds. Without doubt not an amazing time, but undeniably a mental and physical accomplishment that I achieved. I felt the success, but I didn't feel the need to tell many people. Although, ironically, I am telling people now.

Each task I felt that same success, not world-beating times but achievements all the same. Throughout the month, I completed a total of 19 workouts between training for and completing the challenges. This came at a time when I was finding exercise a chore and a bore. The setting of said goals and challenges are what makes exercise interesting for me. If you are struggling for the motivation, set yourself some unusual and interesting challenges. And go do them. The result will be a sense of purpose and achievement in exercise along with the bonus of looking good in the mirror. Maybe pick things you are bad at and get good at them. The healthiest bodies are generally those who have an all-round fitness in many disciplines.

The habit of exercise has been laid out in two good books, 'The Power of Habit' Charles Duhigg and 'Atomic Habits' James Clear. I would recommend reading both. The key information I took from these books is the implementations of habit are crucial in a person's quest for fitness. Exercise can be routine, part of your day that requires no thoughts, just following your daily journey like you do when you brush your teeth or make your coffee. My recommendations are that you replace a current bad or lazy habit with a good one. What I have done is replace my couch time with exercise, I must exercise before I can chill on my couch. So now I come home from work and have my trainers on in no time and hit the gym. It's automatic, I don't think about it, I have made the decision a long time ago that this is what I do every day. This is my daily habit. It almost takes more energy not to do it anymore. Ensure when it comes to exercise that it fits in easily with the flow of your day, it works as part of your routine. You don't have to go far off your daily journey to complete the workout. Make it part of the routine and make it easy to do. If you don't have a current daily routine or you are travelling you can still do it, any spare 20 minutes is enough to blast out a hotel room workout or a run. See my website for some 20-minute workouts you can do anywhere.

Exercise accountability buddies. This is an amazing tool in your prevention of being a waste of a human body. Commit to another person or people, that you will inspire them, and they will inspire you to challenge yourself and your body to achieve greatness. Together you and your accountability buddy should set out set times and days each week when you will exercise together. This allows you to form a sort of verbal contract and you don't want to let the other person down. This will give you and your buddy the extra motivation to get up early and go run because you know he is waiting for you to start. Or after work put on your gym gear because you know that she will be at the spinning class keeping you a bike beside her. This kind of relationship is healthy and amazing if you can find it. Even if you can't meet the person for every or any workout, just having someone to help you keep to your goals is a tool in the quest for a body that functions at its optimum level. If you don't even live in the same country you can still tell the buddy your schedule and times. After the week you check in and talk about how it all went. Maybe a bit of healthy competition can be involved to push each other towards a similar goal.

Commit to yourself. This exercise thing is going to help elongate and improve your life. There is no doubt about the benefits. Make a commitment to your future self to move. The more you move now, the more you will move in later life. When you're older, you won't be frail, you'll be strong and healthy because you made these decisions now about your life. Consciously think about what kind of person you want to be when you are ten years older than you are today. Once you have thought about it, set in place a plan to become that person. What do you need to start doing this week? What is the first step towards being that person? Take it.

One common mistake, amongst those who are exercising to lose weight, is the classic spot fixing method. I don't like the fat around my waist so I will do some crunches approach. I will do so many crunches that my fat will burn off from this area. This is a misconception. You can't lose fat specifically in one area, your body does not work like that. As mentioned earlier, you will lose fat only in a caloric deficit which will be easier to be in with exercise. The exercise you do may stimulate muscles in a certain area to breakdown, repair, and grow but the fat in that area is not being used specifically. Unfortunately for those in search of spot fixing, your body will lose fat from everywhere and more than likely where you store most will be the last to be removed. Whole body exercise, including weight training, stretching, and cardio is the best way to go to lose fat and achieve the sought after 'toned' look. And yes, weight training for both men and women.

Another common mistake--this one made by women specifically--is that weight training in women will lead to them becoming some sort of Incredible Hulk type character that you may have seen in bodybuilder pictures. This is a myth. Women do not naturally produce the testosterone to gain these muscles. The bodybuilding women who maybe freak you out, take testosterone. Women should not be afraid of weight training; it is so useful in giving you that 'toned' (I hate that word) look that women strive for. Without weights, this won't happen. If you are a cardio queen, you will get a stick-like look without the muscle to shape your arms and legs. It's that subtle muscle look that is the toned look so sought after. These are only external benefits. The benefits that should be put above all is health. A healthier you is harder to kill. But each to their own. Weight training has been proven to help men, women, and the elderly maintain bone, joint and muscle health. If it's not for you, it's not for you, I don't particularly like cycling, it's not for me. Find your exercise thing or things, and just do it. (I think Nike will sue me now).

Exercise is a privilege; I remember a story a Pakistani friend of mine told me once of his experience in a bathroom before he completed his second IronMan triathlon. The race was happening in Dubai, a city of extreme wealth but also some extremely tough working conditions that migrants from places like Bangladesh, Nepal and Pakistan must face. The story was two

Pakistani toilet cleaners were speaking to each other in Urdu, which my friend was able to understand but they didn't know. They were saying these rich people's jobs must be too easy to have the time and energy to do a race like this on their day off. If we think about the fact that many of us are overweight when there are people living in the world who are dying of starvation. Many of us have lots of free time but are too lazy to exercise when others can't because they are just far too exhausted working 7 days a week 12 hours a day like the Dubai Toilet cleaners. To put things in perspective, take a long look at yourself and think how lucky you are to have choice in what you eat and have the choice to exercise. You are not so exhausted from work that you can barely stand, you are, and I am at times just lazy. It's time to exercise your privilege literally and do it because you can.

Go exercise in exciting places and don't even think of it as exercise. It can be just living. Going hiking in the mountains, swimming under a waterfall, surfing at dawn. The world is your oyster, go out and see it, go for a run or walk in nature. Go camping in the forest or desert. Embrace the opportunities the world gives you to move. Enjoy the privilege of your life and body by using it. Exercise and fitness shouldn't be a chore (oh that's easy for him to say) it's a spice of life. When you have a weekend free, go make an adventure out of exercise. Because you do your 3 runs during the week, you can now run along the beach and grab an ice-cream after. You do your cycling in the gym so you can cycle into the countryside and stop at that little café you like. This is your freedom because you are fit and healthy from exercising and fueling your body correctly. With fitness, you have opened the door to adventure, and adventure is at the heart of experiencing this earth in all its wonder.

11 HAPPINESS IS WITHIN

What is happiness? Is it possible to be happy all the time? Why don't we mush together all the things that make us happy and do them every day? This would make every day perfect, easy. We literally only live in the moment, yet our moments are taken over by the worries for the future and regrets from the past. The only thing you are in control of is the right now. The right now is where we always live, that is why we must appreciate the right now. What is brilliant about this right now? Too often, people do not appreciate what they have until they have lost it. They cannot take the joy in right now when they have it. Think of all the things that if you lost them from your life now, you would be devastated. Are you even fully appreciative of them now? For me, I am thinking about people when I say this to myself, and I constantly must remind myself to enjoy them while they are in my life. Who gives a fuck about trivial work things when what really makes you appreciate life is love?

Does this mean that those who live in the moment cannot have goals? Do mindful people spend all day eating doughnuts and hugging their mothers? Can you set mindful goals? It's not as if being mindful and being present means you don't think there is a tomorrow. People who live in the now do, of course, set goals and achieve amazing things, they are just aware of the present as they do it. They are conscious to enjoy the process. Setting goals where you dismiss loved ones as you suffer daily to achieve a materialistic target might be an example of someone who isn't a mindful goal setter.

Nothing gets done when no risk is taken in your life. One who isn't a risk taker is one who has not seen or imposed their life limits. The comfort zone is where most of us spend our lives. This is natural. From hunter-gatherer times we are conditioned in a way to embrace comfort when we have it. It goes against our ancient DNA to take risks. That's totally unscientific but you know what I mean. The risky ones back when we dragged around baseball bat type mallets behind us were the ones who died as teenagers. Now what we have perceived as risks are not actual risks in the life-or-death scenario. A risk, now, is asking someone on a date, posting something 'real' on social media, or going on a thoroughly safety-inspected roller coaster. Fuck that for risks, we are easily able for these bullshit risks. You are a conscious human, take a plunge into the unknown, try things, don't just sit on your ass and say 'someday I will do that'. The old question of when are the two best times to plant a tree? Answer, 20 years ago or right now.

I wish I had started going to the gym last year and then I would be in shape. I wish I had started my master's degree two years ago, I would have it now. I wish I had stopped smoking 10 years ago. You see where this is going? Take the step now so the future you can look back and say, "Hell yeah! I started last year and look at the progress now." Whatever your goal is, plan to start now, a step, the first step. Maybe you don't have a specific goal yet, so start with a step to investigate what you might like to do, experiment doing things and taking risks.

Angry. An angry man will write the greatest speech he will ever regret. The need to be right, or in the right is the flamethrower that will bring anger to full flame. People think they are right in conversations, discussions, and arguments, ad nauseum. Of course, you think you are right about almost everything you do, you can defend all your stances and decisions like some kind of warrior going to battle. Even when you are wrong you are right with the classic, 'yes but' response. "You left the door unlocked" "yes but I thought you were coming home at 4, you didn't tell me". Boom, the 'switcheroo' you have turned it on them. Being right is part of the human psyche, an easy lazy fall back, while admitting you are wrong, or have made an error and doing so without a fight or comeback, is very much from an alien planet. It is a skill and a wonderful trait that you should practice.

How many times at work have you been so sure you are in the right on some issue and it boils and steams inside you? You fume at work that Susan didn't do the thing the right way and now it is more work for you. Fuck you Susan, making my life more difficult, I am covering up for your rubbish. You are so angry about this extra work caused by someone else's incompetence. You are in the right. No doubt, you are the most amazing employee on the planet without a single mistake or error (loser).

Your reaction is all you can control in life; you cannot control what the world does to you, you can only control what you do back. You can go to the shelf of reactions in your mind every time something like this happens to you. So many of us choose from the reaction shelves marked "Over" and "Angry". We jump to these reactions with no thought, no conscious choice to be made. You have ruined your own day by making this choice. The mistake Susan made is not going to change but you have chosen the reaction as a negative angry one. Maybe that angry reaction will follow you home and you choose once again to react negatively at home when your husband puts his feet on the table. The negativity and anger are compounding, you're fuming, you go to bed and cannot sleep, thinking about how you have been so right in these two incidences, Susan is incompetent, your husband is a slob. You have judged and sentenced them both to not being worthy of the brilliant you.

Just a couple of things: Susan's grandfather had just died, hence the sloppy work as she was obviously distracted (but you were too wrapped up in your ego to notice she was upset) and your husband needed to elevate his leg as his knee was giving him trouble (of course the inanimate material table is more important?). Technically, at some level, you were right in both these incidences, but instead of a jumping angry judgmental reaction, you easily could have chosen, with free control over yourself, a slower, egoless response. Even if Susan was just being lazy and your husband was just relaxing, how does the anger serve you? They are trivial in the scheme of things. Why do you give such a fuck? Control your reactions as a conscious human. Pause before selecting from the angry shelf of response.

Another way to control anger is to put yourself in someone's shoes who is giving you advice, what would you tell yourself? This different sense of perspective on the cause of your anger may well lead you to replacing the anger with an answer to it. All strategies to contain and control anger use that fact that anger is a choice as their basis. Almost always when we react angrily, we regret the action either instantly or after a short period of time. We become annoyed with ourselves for our reaction to our friend when they hit a nerve. We end up suffering because we begin to think what others thought of our negative reactions. All of this can, of course, be avoided.

Whatever the question is, I find it hard to believe the answer ever is anger. It really can make an idiot out of us. We choose when and how to react; can you stop yourself making these negative reactions is the question you must ask yourself. At least you need to try and come up with a strategy when you are in certain situations. The old saying of 'sleep on it' is best when reacting to messages and emails which have annoyed us. Maybe even write what you want to send through gritted teeth but do not press send--give it some time, even think about what type of response you hope to get from your reply. Are you about to start a cycle of regret and stress through an angry exchange?

Everyone's decisions when they interact with you comes in some part from a thought process where they are in the right. They, maybe with flawed logic, have concluded that sending this email, message or proceeding with a course of action is the right thing to do. Remember that people generally are not out to get you, they are just looking out for their own interests. Everybody thinks they are justified and in the right. Just breathe and remember three things--you could be wrong, you can choose your reaction, and who really gives a fuck?

The reason why I am so interested in anger as a response is because I am conscious of my own anger. It is not something that has been a problem for others, I don't think, but it was a problem for my happiness. I would be pissed off with the slightest little thing in my life going wrong. I was always right. I became aware of it. I was ferociously competitive when it came to coaching. I would get so angry I could feel my head expanding when shouting followed by a splitting headache. It's funny to look back now, but I got myself so worked up over something so unimportant in the scheme of things. Coaching, along with work, driving, shopping, talking and breathing would be sources of anger for me. Every single time, it was a choice I selected. I gained nothing from being angry I just worked myself up. Now I choose differently, not always, but I am getting better--perspective and being conscious of it has helped me immensely. At the end of the day, almost nothing is worth my anger, because anger negatively effects my wellbeing and I want that more than anything.

The anger leads nicely into the Sleepless Night Thinking Syndrome (that's the medical term, honest). Over-thinking can make a problem ten times greater than it is and thinking at night when we are trapped in our quiet, dark spaces can make it one hundred times the problem it was. It is dark place inside the mind loop of the nighttime thinker. Mountains made from molehills and we know this as we think about it, but we ignore logic at this time of night, we spin around and round in our head the events of the day that caused the thinking. This is where being used to empty time during other parts of your life will come in useful, as discussed in Chapter 5. Once you can control your mind when you are aware of it you will be able to easily cope with these problems, but if you're like me, and not quite at that 'Zen' level yet, it can be difficult.

The first thing to do in this case is perspectivize it (totally a word). You know that at night you blow things out of proportion and it is difficult to get perspective, but you need to compare it to a previous time that this has happened to you. Focus the mind and seek from your memory the last time this happened and how did it all play out after the sleepless night? Two things could happen here: one, you can't remember the thing that caused it the last time; hence it didn't matter a shit and you feel relief that the last time it was so insignificant that you can't even recall it. The other thing is that you do remember, and without fail, you remember that the result was better than you had imagined it would be in the deep dark nighttime place.

So now you have got a bit of perspective, how do you get to sleep? A lot of theories on this, from getting up, breathing techniques, reading, and mediation. The one thing we all know not to do but we probably do it anyway, is the nighttime reach for the phone. The lazy addiction is back, there is no solution to your sleep in the phone, and you know it, but it's a habit cycle you are in. My personal strategy when the thinking is becoming too intense and I am wide awake with worry is to get up and write. I leave the bedroom and turn on a light, sit on the couch and write the problem and my solution. The solution will be the steps I am going to take when I wake to solve it. If you don't want to get up, then just focus on these steps in your head as a solution. You will do them tomorrow. If you must pick up your phone, and for most of us realistically that is what we do, stay away from the issue that is troubling you. If it is a lack of text back, avoid the texts. If it is work email, avoid going over this, etc. etc. make this a contract in your mind before you pick up the phone.

There is no major solution to sleep problems in the paragraph above as I am no sleep expert. If you need more information on this, be a conscious choice-making human and read a book on it. A tired body and mind need rest. I notice when I haven't exercised both body and mind every day, I find sleep so much more difficult to achieve. The routine and habit of going to bed is the other thing that can affect sleep. Staying up late at night leads to a cycle of staying up late at night. The human body needs 8 hours of sleep, it is not a sign of strength to use less than this. Less than 8 hours is detrimental to your health. Let's look at some things to help with sleep:

Exercise the body, push your body each day so it has used up all the energy it has and craves slumber but do not do this just before bed, a bit like caffeine below, you can experiment but I like at least 2 hours to unwind after exercise before I can sleep

Exercise the mind, do not just watch hours and hours of mindless screen rubbish, test your mind and create something, write, read, do crosswords, math puzzles, etc. Your mind has energy like your body-- if you don't use it during the day, it will want to run around different thoughts at night

Have a routine for bed, we all know this, a set time, a set procedure, one that has worked for you, time, temperature, bed comfort, no blue lights etc. make it relaxing in nature, slowing you down, take your time doing it.

Get up early consistently and work the mind or body, getting up early will help with routine which sleep loves, and taxing your body or mind will start your metaphorical engine for the day which will need rest at the end of the day.

Avoid naps, no matter how tired you are, power through that afternoon slump, go for a walk, exercise, cook, do something on your feet to reenergize. Napping is out of routine and it confuses some of us. If you can nap and still get a good night's sleep then go for it but if you are struggling to sleep at night and you are a nap fiend, stop it immediately.

Caffeine cut off, if you love caffeine and need it to wake, like me, you need a caffeine cut off in the evening. You can experiment with this, but I cut it off 4 hours before bed which for most is too close to bedtime, so you can figure this one out yourself with experimentation. My father can have an espresso and can hit the hay instantly, my mother can't have caffeine after midday. Different strokes, different folks.

Some people don't enjoy experiences. This is the opposite to mindfulness, where people are in an experience but not in the experience. You are out for an amazing meal with your partner, but you spend the whole time bitching about price of the house water. You are on a beach on holidays, but you spend the time worrying about the office. You are sitting in a comfortable chair in silence and you are thinking about some bullshit email you got earlier. Remember, if the something you are stressing and worrying about now is something that will be forgotten by you and all in a week, that shit is nothing to stress over. It will go away. It will. Stop and smell the roses, enjoy time with people. Think about the number of times you have been in the presence of a friend and you have spent a portion of the time with them on your phone. You are out for a meal and you are scrolling to Instagram looking at some fitness influencer trying to sell you fucking 'fit tea'. Be present in your experiences, enjoy what is happening now. Now you are reading or listening, well done, enjoy the fact that you have chosen to do this and improve you instead of watching some mind-numbing rubbish. Enjoy life, truly enjoy today, enjoy the fact that you woke up, enjoy food, enjoy risk, enjoy who you are, and enjoy the journey you are on. Time is too short not to.

Should a person judge another? It is so easy to judge, and we have been conditioned to constantly judge. From the caste system in some cultures to the nightclub line in others, people judge people every day. Think for a moment of someone who judged you on an occasion. Maybe you were having an off day or maybe it was a first date and you were nervous. Your mind is conditioned to judge; you have been brought up on a diet of reading books by covers. I know what his story is, when you see his tattered clothes, or I know what she is like when you see her Botox forehead. What the fuck? Seriously the society we live in is so quick to judge, so quick to sum up a person based on a snapshot. I think I just judged society, God damn it. I know that this is a problem I have too-- throughout this book, I have judged others, it's so easy to fall into the trap, but I know I judge less than I used to and will strive to continue that trend. Please bear with my faults.

The conclusion: appearances trumps the depth of a person. If you could see what people are made of (talents, loyalty, honesty, humor, ego) in a snapshot instead of body and clothes, what would your reaction be? Earlier in this book I have written about overcoming this judgement by looking at first impressions. Was it wrong to even have that discussion? Should we care if people judge us? We can control how much, if at all, we judge others, especially those we don't know. Take a step back from the conclusions you might be about to lazily jump to and just let people be.

Practicing daily gratitude has been shown to have a strong correlation to improving a person's wellbeing. Maybe it is time you bring gratitude more into your life? It is too easy to ignore it as a practice, but it can be so valuable for your overall health and reducing stress.

5 practices to bring gratitude into your life

Just write it down now, or sometime soon what you are grateful for, no judgements, you can scrap it afterwards, just create a list. Do it when you feel you least would like to do it, when you are at your lowest may be the time you need it most.

Write it down as a practice in the morning, it sets a positive tone for the day, have a routine of writing down what you're grateful for, keep a gratitude journal for this, and use it to look back on.

Gratitude letter: write and send a letter to someone you are grateful for, tell them why and expect nothing in return, just say you are grateful, fill someone's bucket.

Gratitude phone call: have what you want to say written down and call someone or leave a voice note or text saying why you are grateful for them and what they have done for you.

Gratitude notes: the little things are sometimes the most powerful. Little handwritten thank you or gratitude's are amazing ways to make someone else's day, you noticed what they did maybe when others didn't.

Start a journal. It will be the most interesting book you will ever read. It is a cleansing and reflective process, something that will chart your growth and progress in life. Maybe it will be the shoulder to cry on that you need, you spilling your guts and thoughts out onto the page. Puke up your inside feelings onto a sheet of paper. A friend of mine once said, vomit on the page until it is full, i.e. keep writing, even complete garbage, until you have filled the page with your random thoughts and happenings. This method is for those who say, "ah I have nothing to write about today, I don't know what to say". I would use this technique with my school classes and after a while, the vomit would become something that was more deep, clear and useful because they had overcome the journal writer's block.

One of the things I have been guilty of is comparison. It has affected my happiness and job satisfaction. On two levels I would compare: the first being the amount of work other employees would do and the second being the amount they would get paid in comparison to me. I let my ego creep into this, as I allowed myself to think that my work was somehow better than another's. I had judged these others as a poor employees, based on anecdotal evidence at best, let's just say it wouldn't stand up in court.. I also thought I was putting in so many more hours and effort than others. I couldn't confirm this, I just felt I was. Although this would totally be at odds with my own theory of outcomes versus time spent. More time spent does not necessarily mean more work completed.

It would annoy me to compare myself to others, I would never consider that maybe they were more efficient than me, maybe they worked more from home and maybe they were just plain better at their job than me. My ego would not let me go there. Instead, I compared myself favorably and became bitter.

However, what if I was right and they were an unmotivated, struggling and lazy employee, so what, why does it affect me and my work? Maybe they have it right and don't emphasis the importance of work in their lives. It shouldn't have bothered me. Maybe if I was the boss, it might bother me but that's someone else's job to be bothered by unproductive workers, not mine. Also, if I am so great an employee, why am I not helping said underperforming employee? I instead of being a good human being making my colleague and myself feel better by helping him, I let him continue to suffer and I continue to be bitter. I asked myself what sort of way is that to be a conscious human? I need to be a better person. A better person would help not compare.

The major comparison I see in the world today is the comparison of money. "Mo money mo problems?" Going back to my work comparison, I used to look at the people who I knew got paid more than me and did some form of money divided by work completed comparison. This calculation would lead to a distinctly lemony result, one bitter guy. As you might know by now I am big believer in outcomes to check productivity of a worker rather than time spent at work. So, I am looking for visual proof of someone's work even though they didn't have to answer to me. I wouldn't be privy to their achievements, I just felt that I deserved to be earning more than them.

Another spiral away from my own happiness by comparing myself to others. Never once would I compare myself to someone who got paid less than me. As with most people's comparisons, we only compare upwards, we never compare with those where we would come off as the overpaid, less efficient, lazy, and the lucky one.

If you are going to compare, compare to someone who you have been luckier than in life. That'll get you back to feeling grateful for your life. Start to compare yourself to someone you know at work who works harder than you but gets paid less. Start to compare yourself to someone who lives in squalor while you live like a comparative king. You see where this is going. Compare yourself to someone who is less fortunate than yourself, feel how lucky you are in life. You are lucky you are more fortunate than someone. The very fact you can read makes you more fortunate in your education than 15% of the world's population. What to do with this information? Let it set you free from the comparison loop of bitterness; when you are aware of your luck, allow it to fill you with gratitude for your life. Embrace the luck you have and allow yourself to use it as a tool for your happiness. To sum up – you are one lucky fucker.

Those people who go a step further and allow comparing to be a steppingstone to help those less fortunate in some way, are truly reaching a new level of being a great human by giving back to humanity. Back to the old saying of a great society is one where old men plant trees for which they will never have the pleasure of sitting in the shade of. A great, conscious human will help those less fortunate than they are without the need for recognition or thanks just because they are aware of their own fortune in life and that is enough. I need to work on this, my laziness prevents me from achieving this, but hopefully someday soon I can improve on this, can you?

Comparisons often affect our happiness because we perceive the person who has something we want as getting it easy or being luckier than ourselves, for example:

Amazing house – we think inherited, but they worked 18 hours a day for 10 years and continue to do it, so it affects their personal life and relationships.

Amazing body – we think genetics, actually they have consistently put in effort in the gym and committed to a long-term nutrition plan which they have stuck to while we eat the pizzas and drink the beer screaming, "that guy is on steroids"

Amazing job – we think "lucky", got promoted because she kisses ass – actually she studied hard and got a master's degree in night school while you watched Netflix and frankly, she interviewed better because she spent 6 hours practicing the night before while you did an hour you thought would be good enough.

Amazing relationship – we think she is only with him for the money – he is an attentive, funny, caring, and loving husband. He puts in effort into his relationship. When they dated to begin with, he dressed well, spoke passionately about his interests and actively listened. When you dated the girl of your dreams you were late, spoke passionately about Game of Thrones, and came across as self-centered.

Amazing life – we think, if only I had the time – actually she makes the time, she has a routine that allows her to do everything she wants, to hit the gym after work , to meditate before work and plan a trip every weekend to do something she is passionate about, she is conscious in this world.

Do you compare yourself to others? Who doesn't right? Ah, look at him with his perfect life and house. I heard a story recently about a young boy who jumped for joy after getting the result of his mathematics test, a 92%. Unbelievable, wow, he had worked hard for it and was utterly delighted with the result. The boy asked his friends what did you get? what did you get? and what did you get? I got 57%, I got 77% and I got 94%. The smile vanished the jump was reduced to a slump the joy was gone; someone had beaten him. The kid was incredibly happy until he realized someone else had done better than he.

Relate this to your current life; you are very happy with your pay packet until you see Sarah in accounts earns 5% more, you are happy with your house until you see then the Smiths down the road have just installed a new barbeque, you are happy with your children's college acceptance until you see the neighbors kids are going to Oxford, you are happy with your choice of partner until Louise's husband gets her a bouquet of flowers and you are happy with your 5km run until you see on social media Mark has run 10km. What are you doing to yourself? Comparing situations and snapshots of others' lives to your own and affecting your happiness negatively.

So much of this can be avoided once you are aware you are doing it. If something is an achievement it is an achievement even if someone else has done something more impressive in the same field. If you have improved yourself from yesterday to today in any task, it is an achievement no matter if someone else is further down on that path or not. The journey of 1000 miles starts with a single step is one of the most used but true statements of all time. But also true is that after 300 miles, there is a hurdle, after 500 miles, there is a fork in the road. Left is an easy paved 'give up' route and right is a thorn-covered, potholed track of hard work and improvement. If you start something there will be hurdles and easy quit options, you must be aware that this is what the people you are comparing yourself to have often faced and overcome. They have overcome the laziness gene rooted in us. You must also choose the determination to continue. You are your own boss and your own situation master, looking at others' good fortune and comparing yourself to anyone other than yourself (and you know this before I say it) is totally and utterly pointless.

Compare yourself to yourself--are you an improved person? Every one percent is an achievement, you can only be better than your past self. You cannot be better than anyone else. You don't know their struggle. You also don't know what they feel or what they did to get to where they are. Be a better you than you were yesterday. Compare on these terms.

Remember these 5 things that can take from your happiness, don't be lazy you are in control of them.

1. **Criticism**
2. **Complaining**
3. **Anger**
4. **Comparing**
5. **Judging.**

12 GROWING THE MIND

Will we all lie on our deathbeds with regret for talents and interests we didn't pursue? No matter what the age or circumstances, only you are to blame for not following up on this. Why not start now? Yes, sign up for a course in modern art appreciation, guitar lessons, car maintenance, personal training, barista skills, or Montessori education. Acquire the skills become a better you. Do not fear failure, fear being someone who never tried.

'Your body is not a temple, it's an amusement park, enjoy the ride' Anthony Bourdain. Although maybe not the ideal role model for mental or physical health, the premise of his statement rang true to me. I want to see what my body can do while enjoying the journey, the tastes and the experiences along the way. Why not try the local food that you have never heard of? At some stage someone hadn't tried pizza before, someone hadn't tried a watermelon or hadn't had ice cream. Imagine the joy and wonder of tasting these foods for the first time as an adult. It's possible to experience new amazing tastes when you travel, maybe not all of them will as euphoric an experience as tasting ice cream for the first time, for every ice cream there is a turnip, but every unique taste you find when traveling is a joy, a talking point and a new life experience. Don't always choose the lazy option of what you have at home, go on live on the edge a little.

Some people aren't interested in educating themselves post-high school or college. Is your brain then a stagnant pond rather than a rushing river? You can invest some of your time into your continued lifelong education. All learning doesn't have to be university-driven. Sometimes, learning from people who are practicing, not a professor who is preaching, can be a better method of learning. Maybe you can use online resources to study, watch lectures when you are using your screen time. You won't get a nice certificate in scroll form at the end of it, but it might be a more useful and authentic experience.

Formal education is a system not without its flaws. When I was in teachers' college, most of my education lecturers had not been out in the education field (teaching) in almost 10 years. Some of the people who were teaching me how to teach had never been employed as a teacher? How is this possible? Listen to Sir Ken Robinson, he has some very interesting points to make about the current education systems around the world. I have my opinion on the education system, it is not perfect but it is mine. I have been constantly changing it and it will have changed slightly since I have written this book. As the saying goes 'When intellects argue, both leave with different opinions than when they enter'. Open your mind to both sides of every discussion and opinion. Neither mine nor anyone's opinion offers a perfect solution on a complicated topic such as education. Try not to fall into the trap of one-sided thinking, it as you might have guessed is the lazy option.

One-sided opinions are everywhere you go. Failure to view from both sides and only from a single source is an issue that is especially prevalent in the modern age of biased information. Every story has two sides, every political debate, minor argument and discussion. Think about becoming more informed. Learn more. In order to learn you must be prepared to fail. Something many of us, myself included, are not good at.

The biggest room in the world is the room for improvement. Most people don't want to enter the room, though. If you dig a little into a school system that is set up to allow all students to succeed at everything, pass every grade and every test you can see that every new generation leaving school is set up to give up. There are no participation medals in real life. When the challenge of learning a new thing comes up, such as learning a new language for that trip you are going to take, we start off with all the right enthusiasm. We buy the book, the app and set aside some time to learn. The only problem is when we self-assess our skills, we realize we are failing. A feeling we are not used to because we have been passing everything in life up to this point. Good job! We have tried something new, something that we wanted as a new skill, but we have fallen at the first hurdle. This shit is difficult, I am getting nowhere, I can't remember any of the words, language isn't my thing. The growth mindset is thrown out the window with this failure to pass your own expectations.

This is the point instead of blaming Ms. Jones in Grade 7 for being nice to you and allowing you to pass the spelling exam, you look in the realism mirror. You are not looking for perfection immediately, learn from the failure and strive for progress. Did you learn a little bit of Spanish? Yes? Well then, strive to learn another little bit tomorrow. Bit by bit, you will get there. Be brave and to keep trying to learn. You are the one who wanted this skill, why give up when it gets slightly difficult? Embrace that new challenge and set your goals step by step to overcome it. Maybe you can adjust your expectations, not of the end goal just how long it will take you. Have the determination to see it through and overcome the nagging lazy gene telling you to give up. Millions of people buy the gym membership but give up when they realize that people who look good in the posters put in years of consistent hard work to get there and not just the month after January 1st. Anything worthwhile takes time and effort but you can get there if you overcome the give up when you don't get instant success hurdle.

On one level, reading is known to be exercise for the mind, but it should be joy of the mind. You can convert text into pictures and videos in your mind with emotions that can make you laugh out loud and cry. You are just reading text. Your pictures in your head although guided by the text are truly unique to you and would not be formed or thought about anywhere if not for the decision to read that book. You want to read but you just don't have time. Well you know that's bullshit anyway. You have time to check Instagram for the 7th time today, you have time to read a book.

Many people say their favorite part of holidays is reading a book or two quietly on a white sand, sun kissed beach. See, you just created a unique picture of that in your mind. Epic, wasn't it? Maybe the favorite part of your day could be the half an hour your set aside to either wind down with the latest romance novel you are reading or to build your knowledge of the world with the history book. Actually, you are reading this now so I should shut up about reading, you know this already, you are doing it, congratulations. Keep it up!

You are going to learn something new; you are going to grow your mind. You have decided you are going to become an expert at Calculus, for some reason, how do you do it? The constant question every teenager and adult has asked themselves. There is no magic formula. The study should be goal-laden and have clear strategies laid out beforehand. You cannot walk into a study session and start it with a 'right, let's do this' and proceed to open the book on the first page. This method follows a well-trodden path to the 6th page where it grinds to an all too familiar halt of frustration. Oh man, I am screwed; this is too much. Make the study a routine, set those small goals, make it comfortable, take notes, give yourself tests where you have the answers and repeat. If that all seems to boring for you, maybe you should learn a party trick.

Party tricks are one way to have fun with your growth mindset. On the shallowest of levels, this could be a seen as a con. A cheap way to gain popularity or attention. Maybe they are but recognize that the best party tricks are not easy. They are a skill that has been honed and practiced to such an extent that it looks effortless.

When I was a teenager, I can still remember the guy that arrived at the night club with a friend of mine; he was nothing exceptional in the looks department and in general was a nice guy, Andrew was his name (no it wasn't but whatever). Later in the evening when the vibe was better, and the dancing had begun, we as intrepid males (with the Dutch courage to back it up) attempted to dance. In my case, the attempt was my well-trodden routine of arms locked at the sides slightly moving to the music with an odd step here and there thrown in for pizzazz. The girls were not flocking to me as you may have expected with such bulletproof swagger. They had their attention on Andrew as he was literally spinning on his fucking head behind me, performing effortless acrobatics perfectly in time to the beat, ugh. Every girl wanted to be with him, and every guy wanted to be him. I am sure some guys wanted to be with him and some girls wanted to be him also, for political correctness. The point of the story is not that Andrew got to go home with Jenny Shaprio, the point is that every human in the room was in awe and recognized at some level that Andrew had a talent and shown his skill and ability with the confidence of someone who had practiced every day to fine tune it.

Party tricks are not cheap. They are what sets you apart from the crowd. It is bringing your skill to a social setting when the time is right to show it. These talents are worked on, not just a spur of the moment thing. Whether it is dancing on your head, mixing drinks, magic, singing a song, playing piano, or making balloon animals. People notice worked-on skills that set you apart from the crowd and make you an interesting person. Someone who has one of these skills is a person who consciously chose to turn off the TV and pursue a skill to the point where it becomes fascinating to others. You can do that, too. Stand out from the crowd. The most underrated party trick is the ability to tell a good story.

"Fine…. Grand…. Good….." these are the days we have. When we are asked to describe the day we just had or the weekend that just went by, we resort to these banal descriptions. Is your day really that shit? Each day has a story to tell even the boring, the benign, could be interesting. The telling of a story is a skill to tune; you can hone yourself into a weaver of the magnificent with the cotton of the ordinary. Just be thankful that you are in the position to tell a story.

Some people decide that their life lacks the sprinkles and shine to impress others. Because of this, they feel the need to lie. This trait can be present in all of us, the need to embellish and impress calls almost daily. Some chose to ignore the call and let it ring out. Others choose to succumb. Filling the listener with bullshit. There is a choice, if you are surrounding yourself with people who aren't impressed with your real you, they are not required in your life. Get used to being comfortable telling your own amazing story.

Long ass boring stories, who wants to read and listen to those? The skill of storytelling is just that, a skill. You just can't master it on the first attempt. How many stories have you told where the second, third and fourth telling improves the delivery? Practice makes perfect said Mr. Obvious. But when you practice the art of storytelling your first telling can be wonderful. You know the pace to speak where to deviate, where to come back, when to repeat, when to fast forward, when to rewind, when to include an impression, when to raise the tone, when to lower it and when to hit the punchline or point. Every story should have an end, a point or a punchline. Bring the listener in by being honest, leaving your ego aside, then bring them on the journey of what happened, stop along the way for a detail or two then increase the pace towards the finish and ease on home with that end punchline.

A storyteller is employable. You may have heard of the classic modern tech company interview strategy of telling the interview panel a story. It's true without a doubt if you can tell a story, you come across as confident, friendly, good communicator, and employable. You can think on your feet, you are engaging and you can sell yourself. This is the most important skill in so many employments, doctors, teachers, salespeople, business and service industry. See it like the most important master's degree that you get from life. If you have it, you are a step ahead on your competition for jobs and relationships. A story ability raises you up that ladder. Practice telling your story and begin with the banal, when you are asked how was your day? "Let me tell you….."

Why do I carry a notebook everywhere? The notebook is a tool of the creative and a friend to the forgetful. I use it for to-do lists, goal setting, writing things that come up in conversations (book suggestions are a usual), diagrams, ideas, notes on documentaries, daydreams, songs, poems, random numbers, names and lots of bullshit. Where would these ideas and creative parts go without the handy notebook to write them? They go to the great graveyard of creativity in the sky, RIP. Go on, get a notebook, small enough for your bag or pocket and just enjoy the creativity down to the last doodle.

On a practical level, a phone can do most of the mentioned things from above, however I feel the personal touch physically writing lends to the thoughts that were going through your head at the time. How you write can evoke the memory more clearly. The to-do list can be physically ticked off, the goals can be edited, the ideas can be expanded, and the drawing can only be done with the feel of paper. I do not say don't use your phone, I only recommend the tactile nature of a notebook to see your creativity flourish. The notebook also can read as very specific type of diary. You can chart your creative flow, see where you let ideas fall away and see where other aspects of your life were created.

The overuse of complicated language in any debate is

possibly a sign of lack of argument. Being a sesquipedalian to sound competent is not a sign of intelligence. See what I did there? Sesquipedalian, look it up. Make your arguments and stories real. The true sign of intelligence is being able to explain the complicated to the ignorant. The best stories are enjoyable to listen to even if the content may be serious or difficult to comprehend. To use the story as a spring board for your ego by criticizing others, exaggerating your input or belittling someone is an automatic turn off for all listeners. Please just don't try and sound uber smart and learned by including your word of the day instead of the obvious word, you sesquipedalian. Apparently my editor has told me this is an adjective and shouldn't be used as a noun, but fuck it, I love living on the edge so it stays.

Is it important to be more conscious about politics? Politics literally rules our lives, it affects health, education, law and infrastructure. Someone must decide on these issues and it is in most countries elected officials who make the decisions. Well, or so we think--watch any political drama or documentary and you see who really makes the decisions behind the scenes. A great deception to the general public is that politics and political decisions are black and white. You have a system where elected politicians must fall into political teams that they cannot stray from when voting on issues. A healthcare bill comes to a vote in your country, it is proposed by the political party in majority power and all that party vote for it, the opposition party or parties all vote against it, the motion is carried, and the healthcare bill is passed. So the system worked and everyone is happy, the pointless vote was a show, the politicians are under pressure of being excluded from the party if they don't follow the rules, the politician won't get elected unless he/she is in a political party so therefore will vote on the issue the way they are told. Ok I have simplified that, but you get the idea.

The unconscious lazy mind thinks that politics is simple, that politicians can just raise their wages, cut their taxes, build that new school, and solve that crime. Those fat cats in Washington. Politicians are human--they are influenced by the perceived simplicity of their own job. They realize that to get elected they must pander to the masses--they will build walls, cut taxes, make jobs and solve crimes. Promise a world of simple, yet economically complex, campaign slogans. Then they get into power after all the promises are made and go about reneging and changing each one, claiming the issue is more complex than just building, cutting, making and solving. Of course, they knew this on the campaign trail, but no politician ever got elected on a sensible ticket of what would be good (but unpopular) for the economy and country. 'We may raise or cut taxes totally depending on how the economy preforms in that fiscal year' would see that politician watching Everybody Loves Raymond on Tuesday mornings in his boxers instead of wearing a power suit behind his mahogany desk watching Fox and Friends.

To think that a political decision such as raising and lowering taxes is anything other than a hugely complicated multi-faceted issue based on predictors and financial modeling is an ignorant approach. Who makes these decisions should be economists and not politicians. The same politicians who have promised unsustainable tax cuts to fool the uninformed voter. Voting for politicians is ingrained in one-sided thinking. Elections are not even about the policy anymore-- it's like following a sports team. If you have become entrenched in a political leaning you will agree with everything that has been decided by that side and the other side are to be scorned at their every turn.

The idea here is about informing yourself on politics as a hugely complicated web of law, economics, debate, and posturing. Politics is more than slogans and perceived power. More than a left or right question, do you follow the political party because you truly have decided consciously, or have you had that decision made for you by your upbringing? Democracy is great and all but sometimes it can lead to an oversimplification of politics which gets voted upon by an underinformed population. This has led to the rise of the celebrity politician who is recognizable therefore voteworthy in some people's mind because they 'like' him/her. Be conscious when you vote for candidates and go beyond the waffle, false promises, and celebrity. I would like the candidates to take some form of IQ test and have the result written on their ballot paper--wouldn't that be a refreshing piece of information to know? That will never happen. Shouldn't the President or leader of any country be an intelligent human? Shouldn't the leader be well read? How is this not a prerequisite? There is no interview for the most important job in the country, no entrance exam, just a 'Hey, I recognize your face and you say down with taxes, I don't like taxes, so you are hired' approach.

13 UH OH, RELIGION

Judgements again, why with the judgement already? Who is to judge a person based on religion, race or circumstances? People have been on different journeys than you, they have grown up in unique circumstances and each person should be allowed to have their own set of beliefs and faith. Religion is a topic that always courts criticism, judgements, and even war. It is not for me to say whether religion is right or wrong or which religion is the correct path to take. If you choose to believe or have faith, then go for if it. If you haven't, then go for that. Unfortunately, way too many people give a fuck about what others think. They become critical of those who don't agree with their way. Have they fully informed themselves on the religion they are criticizing? Or do they fully understand their own religion?

Religion is said to have been created at a time when people needed something to believe in, to keep order amongst the savages. Where would the world be without it, no one knows of course. Maybe without religion we would all be in the land of butterflies, unicorns and tra la la or maybe we wouldn't have a set of morals that guide every human to do right. I don't know. I would like to think humans would get to the moral code without the need for religion. I suppose that is why we have laws. I'd also like to hope in the future religion would not be used as an excuse to judge, exile and even murder, which unfortunately it often has been. Almost all countries have natural laws that are independent of religion. In Ireland, for example, where I grew up, they have been having referendums on formerly religiously imposed laws on Divorce, Abortion and Gay Marriage. Letting the public decide, not something that is written in a book that only some people believe. Do we know enough about religion to live our lives by it?

Take Christianity--do you know why Christians light candles, drink wine and bread at service or read certain prayers? Do you know why Muslims go on Hajj, not eat pork or have a call to prayer? Why do Hindus put a bindu on their forehead? Why do Buddhists burn incense? Why do Jainists not eat living things? These are just the obvious traits, religions have their own scriptures, rights, procedures, and ceremonies. Unless you have delved into each religion, read their scripture and spoken to believers, you shouldn't even have an opinion, much less have judged them. Everyone should have the right to choose their path and faith. Sure, a discussion could be had, but leave your ego at the door, you could be wrong. In every conversation you have about religion always remember you don't need to be right or convince the other person they are wrong. Scientists will admit they cannot explain everything, they have the big bang theory but, what created the thing that was banged? Who the fuck knows?

Are you good because you fear a God or are you

good because you are good? Individual moral code vs religion, what would the world without religion look like, a morally corrupt cesspit of orgy and murder no doubt. We will never know why people are good, but does it rely in any way on religion? The world is full of the religious and non-religious alike committing crimes, some are committing crimes in the name of religion, for example, the Christchurch killings in 2019 and New York 9/11. The question must be why are people good? And why do people do bad things? Are we good because of the fear of what may happen when we die, in other words we would as a part of human nature be 'bad' but because of the threat of post death incarceration in eternal hell (Christian example) we remain good, just chomping at the bit to be bad? The other alternative is that we are naturally good and have within us a moral code free from any religious structure. I like to believe the second option; we don't need religion for moral code. The world has spent thousands of years creating and updating laws to punish those who are not 'good'. We don't need religion for post-death punishment for breaking the code, that is why we have these laws. The question you need to ask yourself is, are you good? What defines good? Somehow you know what defines your good, you have a code of ethics and you follow it.

There is an interesting debate on whether a child should get to choose their religion when they reach a certain age. Surely it is an amazing coincidence, and I am not the first to say this by any means, that if you are born to Hindu parents in India you just so happen to be a Hindu baby, if you are born to Muslim parents in Saudi Arabia you are a Muslim baby and if you are born to Christian parents in America you are a Christian baby. So lucky. Imagine being born in America to two Christian parents and coming out of the womb a Muslim baby, that would be a surprise.

Religion is learned from conditioning the same as your social skills, in the same way someone who is rude in a restaurant thinks they are in the right because they are emulating their rude parents and know no different. People think they are right about their religion as they are conditioned to believe it not choose to believe it. Religion is not necessarily a bad thing, but religious intolerance is. To tell someone else to believe in what you believe is your ego talking; you must be right because it is what you believe. Maybe you have read books on religion and you feel that a person must be made aware of the hypocrisy of their religion. You tell them they are wrong in what they believe. For whose benefit are you doing this? Are they going to be happier knowing that what they have always thought was right was a work of ancient fiction? Or are you going to be happier because you have imposed your ego and shown how smart and well-read you are?

It's a difficult debate, as the more conscious and well-read we become, the harder it may become to subscribe to religion as it has been presented to us from childhood. Before you go preaching from any mountain top, read both sides of the debate on any topic and what you might come to realize is that, as you gain more knowledge, you understand how little you know. That is where the strive for more knowledge should come from-- the more you know, the less you think you know. Be conscious of both your ego and your lack of ultimate knowledge; you are not an expert in a topic until you have fully delved into it. The truly conscious may share what they have read in a book as interesting but will read further books before they can deeply discuss the topic and conclude.

Unfortunately, in the modern world of instant communication we don't have time for that shit, we must respond, be offended and be righteous. During the writing of this book I have changed some of my opinions, maybe just slightly, as I have been reading other books. My final opinion on religion will never be final as I may have further thoughts on it the next hour if I speak to someone, read a book or watch a film. Maybe in my last throes I will have my final say. Until then, I will continue to learn.

Unfortunately, like most children born in the 20th century, my opinion starts with a religious conditioning; I, until 14 years old or so, blindly and unconsciously followed the religion of my parents. I was never given a brochure of religions to choose from when I reached maturity and told 'go on son, pick the best one for you, the one you believe in'. I can't have sex, drink or vote until I am 18 but I can decide on what my afterlife of infinity will be when I am 0?

We don't get a choice in our religious path, as our parents didn't, as our parents' parents didn't, but someone in that line did--someone in our history chose our religion, what made them wiser than us? That choice must have been made with less information than we have now. Maybe they converted under pressure of death? Do you know the story of which one of your ancestors made the choice and why? I certainly don't, and you can't say your family was always part of this religion because all religions have a start date, and before them, there were different religions. Your ancestors could have drifted in and out of religions, had different and of course, no religion. So your great great great great great great great great great great grandfather choose this for you, maybe he was an incredibly wise (pretty great by all accounts) and well-read man or maybe he lived in the same house all his life and didn't have access to Google scholar or Encyclopedia Britannica and he knew of no other religions other than what he heard from a passing preacher. Maybe your family's religious choices were made on a whim, maybe they were made under fear of death and you have followed these without question. Don't look to your parents, they only continued this choice to protect you.

Parents made your choices for you as a child. In the most cases, parents make the choices to protect you and keep you safe. What sort of choice would be allowing your child to be an atheist in Saudi Arabia until they decided themselves? You would be putting your family's health at risk. You could be excluded from the community. People love to be part of the safety and warmth of a community. With these pressures, parents decide for you to go with the flow and keep in the community. It is the protection of the child they have in mind. Are decisions of religion a decision at all if it is exclusion that sways the decision? This goes for every religion; the religious community do not take well to a decision not to indoctrinate a child into their ranks. As many countries have religion at the heart of the community and in some have it as part of the law, going against that would be social suicide, hence the conformity.

In some parts of the world, this chain is breaking, and religion is not central to the community anymore. These countries have put the state and the wellbeing of its people at the center. Maybe they are worse off for this, maybe then these newly-born children will be conditioned without a religion and upon turning 18, will go straight to the local Mosque and ask to be let in. There are at least 12 countries in the world in which over half the population claim to be non-religious, including China, England, Netherlands, Vietnam, Czech Republic and Japan. You would describe none of these countries as being particularly lacking in moral standards or lack of community. Some non-religious find other beliefs to follow that put them in an alternate community, once again looking for that safety in a community. Examples of this are the Humanists, Atheists and even Flat Earthers. The need to belong is strong and people need to categorize themselves. For what reason do we need this? Is it because when someone asks, we have an answer? Is blindly following the lazy option? On a recent form I had to fill in a religiously strong state I was told that I couldn't leave the religion field as a blank. I had to categorize. I had to belong, otherwise I was an unknown, a danger maybe.

The greatest team you may follow, without question, is the religious team you follow. Now in the lead, with 31.5% are the Christians, coming up in second place are the Muslims at 23.2%, and in the bronze medal position, with 15%, are Hindus. Unlike political and sports team leanings, if you want to make a conscious decision about religion it isn't that easy. As mentioned already, you are conditioned without your consent into this faith and belief. You don't get a choice to believe, you're told to believe. In Catholicism, for example, they put in place original sin (on top of the social pressure) so you would have to baptize your baby as soon as possible into the religion so it could go to heaven if it died. You are blackmailing young parents into entering your religion from the start by holding their child's entry into heaven over their heads. Realistically, the only ones that should get into heaven and the only ones without sin are those who are newly born, but no, they saw to it that babies carried sins into the world that only a baptism can remove. There I go judging again. Oops.

Religion, of course, is one of those things that we should therefore look at all sides of the arguments for and against each one before we choose, if we choose at all. Religion for many isn't seen as choice. If you think of choosing, you are rebelling, you could be shunned by community and family. Is the choice of religion not the most important decision there is? Does it not affect the path we go on after we die, as well as our paths during life? Can a switch of religion lead to a different afterlife path than if we stuck with the religion our parents chose for us? Is our life path pre-determined and we shouldn't even bother to question religion and beliefs and should just accept it and get on with it? Ahhhhh, my head hurts. So, consciously the question is, as someone who thinks deeply about the world, should you think deeply and question religion and then make a conscious decision about it?

Do not let your ego take over your thoughts on religion. You do not need to be right in the discussion. If you believe something, you have a right to believe it (although the rights of a human are a social construct, see the book Sapiens by Yuval Noah Harari). Forcing your opinion on others is not what an intellectual would do. The question I once heard known atheist Stephen Fry ask was "How dare you create a world where there is such misery that is not our fault?" when asked what would he say if there was a God and he met him, he was talking specifically about explaining bone cancer in young children. I heard Ricky Gervais describe atheism as not believing in all 3000 different Gods and a religious person believing in 1 and not believing in the other 2999. Is religion an amazing work of fiction generally sourced from the Middle Eastern area of the world? Why was God from all the major religions we believe in obsessed with that area? Did God not care about the Americas? Until more recently or course, in God we trust.

This is not a book to convert or turn people away from religion-- it is more a book to open eyes and ask questions where previously you drifted through life and accepted the side of the story you have always heard. Search out your own truth, the more you know, the less you think you know. I have not studied religion in a great enough detail to say any certainties, science can only explain so much, and still hasn't explained a lot. The reason we have so much faith in religion is we are a species of story tellers. We needed religion to explain so much of the unknown as we developed. Stories evolved to explain the sun and the stars as well as earthquakes, thunder and the tides. A lot of times, these stories were conveniently biased towards the tellers. Research as much as you can before you bow your head in prayer, for picking the wrong team could lead to eternal damnation. Bit of a bummer that.

14 THE IMPORTANT STUFF

Job satisfaction is one of the most important paths to happiness in the modern world. Many people dread the thought of going to work in the morning, others, of course, are in the technically 'Meh' category. Do we have a right to be excited about our work? No, we have no such rights. Who you work for is a choice, that is our right, the right to choose where to work, how to work, if you work at all.

Dread is something that you should reserve for the dentist (maybe) and is not an emotion that should happen very often, if ever. Can you control the dread? Can you decide what you dread? What about the job you go to everyday, do you dread it? The commute? Your boss? Coworkers? The pressure? The mundane? The tasks? If your 9-5 is a major struggle it is time to reevaluate why you are there. Take steps to make it a positive experience. Take pride in your work, I have always found that helping others is the best way to feel good about work. It's kind of a circular effect that you are helping yourself when you help others.

Set yourself goals at work to strive towards--this could help through those shitty lazy days. Form a structured routine to your day that allows you to be productive and remember to switch off when you leave. The great Sir Jon Jones said he would always pick a point on his drive home from work where he would mentally and consciously switch off all thoughts from the workday. You can do that too, if you are allowing yourself to be consumed by thoughts of work all evening and before sleep realize you are still on the clock even though you aren't being paid anymore.

One of my favorite stories I heard Anthony Bourdain tell is the one of the two dishwashers. Two dishwashers started work as young enthusiastic employees of a kitchen in New York. They were given a list of tasks to complete in their shift. The shift started and they decided their best course of action was to work at an efficient steady fast pace and complete all tasks as quickly as they could and then they would be able to relax at the end of the shift. With youthful gusto in a new job, they completed the tasks in double quick time and with two hours left in their shift they had shiny floors, polished silver and folded laundry. They rewarded themselves by sitting down, shooting the shit and enjoying a cigarette. That was until the boss walked in. 'What the fuck are you dickweeds doing?' They explained they had finished all the tasks. 'Well I am not paying you two shits to sit around and have a joke, you're on my time, go wash the fucking floor again". The two newbies re-washed the spotless floor while grumbling and bitching. Guess what the two young enthusiastic employees did the next night? The list of tasks was the same, but the pace of their work was slower and amazingly they finished all tasks exactly at 1am when their shift ended. 'Not on my time'.

This story rang true for me-- with so many jobs, it is not the tasks completed we are paid for really, it is the time we are present at the office, site, kitchen, etc. If you have hired someone to do a job why are they paid for the time, not the job? I am sure you can think of some colleague in your past that would just put in the time and that was enough for them to be secure in a job. They would lack pride and be lazy in their work because the bar was so low, i.e. turn up on time, do enough, and leave when we say you can. It is like a jail or school system all your life.

If you are an employer, you need to value your employees and look out for their wellbeing. A happy and motivated employee will always produce better results in the long run. Some jobs may require a time-based schedule such as nursing, but results-based employment should be employing people on a results basis not just to show up for a set amount of time and do enough. Maybe I am missing something, but it makes sense to me, and I think some companies are moving this way with flexible time and working from home, but it is a slow process. It is very much based on trust: do you trust the employee to work when you aren't physically in the same space?

Education systems need to be revaluated. For a country, it is hugely important to have the right education for its citizens. It should be a high priority for parents or those still in schooling. Even if you are not a parent, you may want to pursue education again at some stage in your life. Universities to a great extent have become money making machines not with the good of nations or people at heart. In many countries, university fees leave students carrying huge debt. These debts mean that once finished university these young people must rush to find jobs to pay it back. Surely, these are the young minds that should be taking risks, trying startups and inventing. Instead, these young people are forced to join a workforce at the paper pusher data entry level and work up. When they finally are debt-free, it is too late to take the risks, they are now probably tied to another debt, maybe a mortgage. All this, so the universities can continue. The accreditation is all they have; you can do everything else they do online.

Writing papers, watching lectures, discussion groups, research all can be done without leaving your laptop. Why do we need these huge fees? It seems outdated and unnecessary to continue with the system as it is. The system is there to serve the universities and keep them churning over the profits, not to serve the people. Unfortunately, employers still look for that accreditation and to get the 'top' jobs, you need the 'top' university degree. This is the universities world, we just live here.

The wonderful world of teaching in an international setting has led me to be sure of what is the best job in the world according to many parents. The best and most sought-after job in the world is a doctor, or wait, is it a lawyer, one of those two anyway. This is the television generation telling the social media generation you need to be the next Dr. Mc Dreamy and Suits guy so I can tell my friends and they will be impressed. My daughter is a doctor. The pinnacle of life, everyone knows what a doctor does and knows that they are a respected member of society perched near the top of our social hierarchy. "My daughter the doctor is marrying a lawyer", oh man, you have fucking won the game of life, can't you see the confetti coming from the ceiling. Hell yeah! All the hard work has paid off, I made my daughter go to medical school. I knew being a dancer was some teenage bullshit and now look at her, marrying a lawyer. Sweet success of life. In your face, fictional family that you hate next door. "So, fictional daughter, when will we meet this lawyer man of yours?" 'Who said it was a man, Dad?'

A doctor is a fine profession, don't get me wrong-- they are amazing, work long hours, deal with unpleasant processes every day, and have a rigorous college process to get to where they are. They are helping one person at a time survive this world. But where is the ranking of professions and jobs that puts them or any job nearer the top? Why are we even ranking these jobs? Well doctors, they help people live who might have died, that is the ultimate job, you are saving lives. Yes they are, but what about the paramedic who saves lives everyday arriving at accidents and performing CPR? What about the microbiologist who develops a vaccine or a cure for a previously fatal disease? What about a detective who solves a case and puts a murderer behind bars, and what about Social Media Influencers who sell fit tea for a 7-day weight loss guarantee?

OK, that was a lot of what-aboutery, but why the clamor for the glamour of certain jobs and professions that often are not that well paid, have high levels of job dissatisfaction and general low levels of happiness? In America, there are 1.3 million lawyers and 1.1 million doctors (how are there more lawyers than doctors, that in itself is crazy). The problem I have is not with the professions here but the people going into the professions are not necessarily the right ones because of social, peer and parental pressures. Some of the brightest and finest are being funneled towards these. Should the brightest minds for instance not be educating the next generation of bright minds? Think of the lost innovations that do not exist because many parents look on existing known jobs as the best and safest bets for their children and hence force them this way. For example, maybe we could have a cure for cancer if we allowed microbiology to sit metaphorically above lawyers when it comes to choosing careers for the next generation.

Doctors, nurses, microbiologists and many others help people and so can you. It doesn't have to be your profession but it can be done in some of your spare time. It could be your hobby, a very rewarding one. Never underestimate what you gain from helping others, it is beyond measure. Everyone has a real ability to help others around them--the poor, the sick, the young, the old, the frail and the challenged. Be realistic about that. You can make a difference try not to be lazy about this.

The question for most people is -- do I want to? If you want to, are you doing it? For the most part, we want to if it is for someone we know and already care about, but maybe not for those we don't know or care about yet. Society makes it OK for you as a citizen to not really care about those you don't know. For instance, I have heard it said that women should cry 'fire' instead of 'rape' if they are attacked. How would you react to someone who is getting attacked is a general question that you will never know how to answer truly unless you are faced with the situation. There is no real way to prove what you would do unless you are confronted with it, but there is a reaction that you will be confronted with every week and possibly day of your life--a person in need of help. I am talking about the person you know who is in a personal struggle and not necessarily a physical struggle. What do you do if confronted by this? You can help. The worst thing about this for me is I know I have been happy with my own laziness when confronted with this, justifying decisions to ignore. I need to be optimistic that my future self will help people more, because I can.

How many people have you helped? As I mentioned before, "a society is said to be great when old men plant trees who shade they know they will never sit in." How many of us can say we have done truly selfless acts in our life not for the rewards they give to us but for no self-gain? How many selfless acts have you performed during your existence so far? Can you list the people you have helped when the time comes, and can you imagine the people you don't know who you have helped? Take satisfaction if you have, seize the day if you haven't and make a difference in the world. Plant a tree.

Remember shit happens, the effect of the outside world on us, we cannot control it, we are not that much in control of our own destinies. So much of our lives are controlled by the unknown. It's like a game of chess or Fortnite (for you young folk); we set out with a strategy and thoughts as how to win and what our moves are going to be. Within two moves, this has all changed and we must now choose a different tactic. All our plans for the game are gone because someone else didn't do what we were predicting they would do. Life is unpredictable like this-- no matter how much you prepare for something, there is always a chance something can go wrong.

Anyone who has watched or played team sports can attest to this; you are training for this one big game, everything is brilliant in training, fitness is amazing, your team is taking all their scores in training, you have the tactics down (everything looks amazing on that whiteboard as the coach goes through it) and you are full of confidence going out onto the field. 3 hours later you are thinking where did it all go wrong? You got hammered, your team looked unfit, the scores were missed, and the tactics were out the window after two minutes. What happened? Life happened, the other team also prepared and were chasing the same outcome, only one team can get that outcome, maybe they were slightly better prepared, maybe it was the referee or maybe it was just shit happens, maybe they got the damn luck. Or maybe they 'wanted it more', this takes luck out of it. From a coach's perspective this is a cheap shot where players are to blame for some sort of mental failing. Everyone sets out to win every game, there must be more to it than wanting it to more. Like in life.

The world only has so many CEO jobs, so many sports winners, so many best-selling authors and so many million-dollar artists, so if you are not one of these, and you were striving hard for it, are you a failure? Were you lazy and the successful ones determined? In small business, the generally agreed upon failure rate after 5 years is 50% and nearly all startups fail to make any profit in the first year. Why so many failures? Surely all these failures wanted to succeed? So, rule that out straight away. A lot of these businesses no doubt put in as much effort as the ones that did succeed. We must ask ourselves why did one succeed and the others didn't? No doubt, the biography of the owner of the success would describe the extra effort and how much she believed in herself, but is this true? It comes down to the question of how much actual control over our own lives do we have?

If we were in full control, maybe everyone would succeed, everyone would be rich, everyone would be happy. Of course, we can make bad decisions, and these could be our downfall not our lack of effort. But like a game of chess, there is another player in fact so many other players. If you are on the way to an important interview and as an amazing driver (we all think we are) we are driving perfectly when 'bang' someone crashes into our rear at a stop sign. Now this bad driver behind isn't even playing the game of you getting your dream job, yet they have basically thrown the chess board across the room and messed everything up. Shit happens, this piece of luck, no matter how well-crafted your interview replies, has meant you missed your once chance interview and has totally changed your entire life. You are not in control of your life; you can have strategies and plans, but they need to be flexible to change. Be conscious about this. Control your reactions to shit happening, this is where true determination can be seen. It is easy to be determined if everything is going your way. It is easy to be lazy when shit keeps happening to you. You are playing the odds of life when you are making goals and routines. You need to be aware that things will knock you off course irretrievably but how you respond and react is key.

'Shit happens' could be the most profound sayings of our existence. As much as we want to be, we are not in control of everything that happens and some people literally do get more luck than us for no reason, not God, not walking under a ladder, not karma just shit, pure brown turds of life. Does this mean we should give up on all our choices and wander unconsciously with no goals and ambitions because the world is conspiring against us? Obviously not. We still can have a huge amount of control over how we spend our time and make our decisions.

What do you have to show for your life's literal work? How productive has my life been so far? Not as productive as it could have been. There is no doubt that reaching someone's potential is impossible. To say I have reached my potential has only shown that you do not believe in your ability to further learn and improve. When a teacher says little Timmy Tom hasn't reached his potential, this sounds fine to us. But delve into the statement, it is dangerous to think that full potential has ever been reached. Good man, Timmy Tom, you have reached your potential.... "Now what Mr. Teacher man?" Eh, go play on your iPad, Timmy Tom. Strive to be productive to create a CV of the mind and body that you are proud of, you can be satisfied with your achievements but can never fully satisfied reach your true potential.

What does a perfect day look like and how much does it cost? A friend of mine asked me this question in a bar in Ho Chi Minh City (Saigon) a few years back. What a great question. What does a perfect day look like for me? So I began to think of all the things I like to do, I needed to stop myself after a minute because I was making a sort of bucket list, with mountains climbed, concerts attended, and seas surfed, and forgetting if I did all three of these things, I would be exhausted and would have also spent 4/5 hours driving. I thought happiness is sharing experiences, a truly perfect day could be free from stress, anxiety, and cost. It would be spending time with those I love and sharing a coffee, food, and stories in nowhere in particular.

The most important thing of all is life-- it is so precious. You must be aware of how feeble we really are as humans; we will all die. A recent experience in Hikkaduwa in southern Sri Lanka has brought this into perspective for me. A normal day by the beach, I grabbed a bit of food and a beer for lunch (we were on holidays ok, don't judge me, it is totally 5 o' clock somewhere) while watching the awesome surfers. Beautiful hot day, sand was melting the bottoms of our feet and vibe was full relax mode. Shooting the breeze with my buddy. Little did we know that the relaxing and paradise-like scene would turn out to be the day we nearly drowned.

After our lunch, we decided to do as we saw others do, and cool off with a quick dip in the sea. Just a quick dip and then off home again. Into the waves we went, diving through and being the cool-ass dudes we were hoping to be. We were not. One minute later we both couldn't find our feet anymore; we were out of our depth and going out to sea with each wave. Both of us are confident swimmers but suddenly we knew we were in the beginnings of our first riptide. Immediately, a scene developed on the beach with people pointing. All the memories of what to do with a riptide came flooding back, but every fiber of my being wanted to be out of the water again. I fought and swam to get back to shore, the panic slowly descending on me like a blanket of despair. I needed to be smart and swim parallel to the shore first. A surfer local came to my rescue just as I had caught a couple of waves back in, he went on to help my friend out. We were safe. Shaken, but safe. Our lives for that fleeting minute were in the balance--had we not realized the danger, maybe we would've been another drowning statistic on that beach.

Later, we researched if there had there been any drownings in that area of late. The answer was an unsurprising yes, it is constant. It is known for having a riptide, but we didn't know, we were ignorant and completely and utterly lucky. Time for perspective. Everyone at some time is close to death, we are all organisms that are quite frail. Embrace your health while you have it. Embrace people when you have them in your life. most of all embrace life, you only get one life and everyone dies, everyone. You must realize, as humans, we are vulnerable. Make yourself harder to kill through prevention, yes, but in general, we have all got to go sometime. When will you go? You don't know, but you do know what makes you happy so find more time for that in your life. Try not to postpone your happiness, it may never happen. Find happiness in each day.

The fragility and shortness of life always hits home most for me when I hear of people diagnosed with cancer and have been close enough to watch the battle they go through. The fight that they put up to just live, to do the thing so many of us take for granted. We bitch and moan about our little problems and let them consume us. In the world there are millions of people who would love to be in our privileged and healthy shoes. Yet how many of us show gratitude for what we have when we have it? Too many of us show anger and regret when we have lost something and not the gratitude when we had it in the first place. Please express your gratitude for what you have today.

When a terminal diagnosis is made, it really seems to focus the mind of the sufferer on what is important in life. When one is put in this position, a clarity seems to arrive. People seem to place relationships and experiences far above money, things and work. When it comes down to the real important things in life, for a person in the position of terminal illness it is not the same as what we place importance on when we make conscious decisions daily. We ignore family, we take friends for granted, we turn down experiences, we work for things and we waste our healthy lives. We are lazy when it comes to what really matters in life. So now might be the time to make a conscious decision to reevaluate the people and the decisions in our daily lives. Spend more time experiencing the wonders of life and the amazing people that are in your life. You could use some of the examples, lessons and methods in this book to improve your life and maybe make each day a better experience. If you don't feel like using my methods because they seem to not serve you, and you are just inspired to be better, then that is awesome too. If you confront your laziness gene and recognize that it is a barrier to your happiness you can take ownership of your life back. Own your life and your decisions. If you take nothing else away from this book take that. Good luck with it.

ABOUT THE AUTHOR

John D. Collins is a teacher, coach, author and founder of FightLaziness.com. He is a graduate of University of Limerick in Ireland with a BSc in Mathematics and Physical Education. He is currently a high school mathematics teacher as well as an author. His writing style is entertaining while informative, trying to get the reader to ask themselves some life changing questions.

In recent years he has focused on developing his time management skills with a more logical and conscious approach to decision making in his life. He has a passion for making every day count and self-improvement. Read his blogs on FightLaziness.com and follow him on Instagram at fight_laziness.

He is happily married to his wonderful wife Rola. Don't forget to make every day the best day ever.

30966512R00102

Printed in Great
Britain
by Amazon